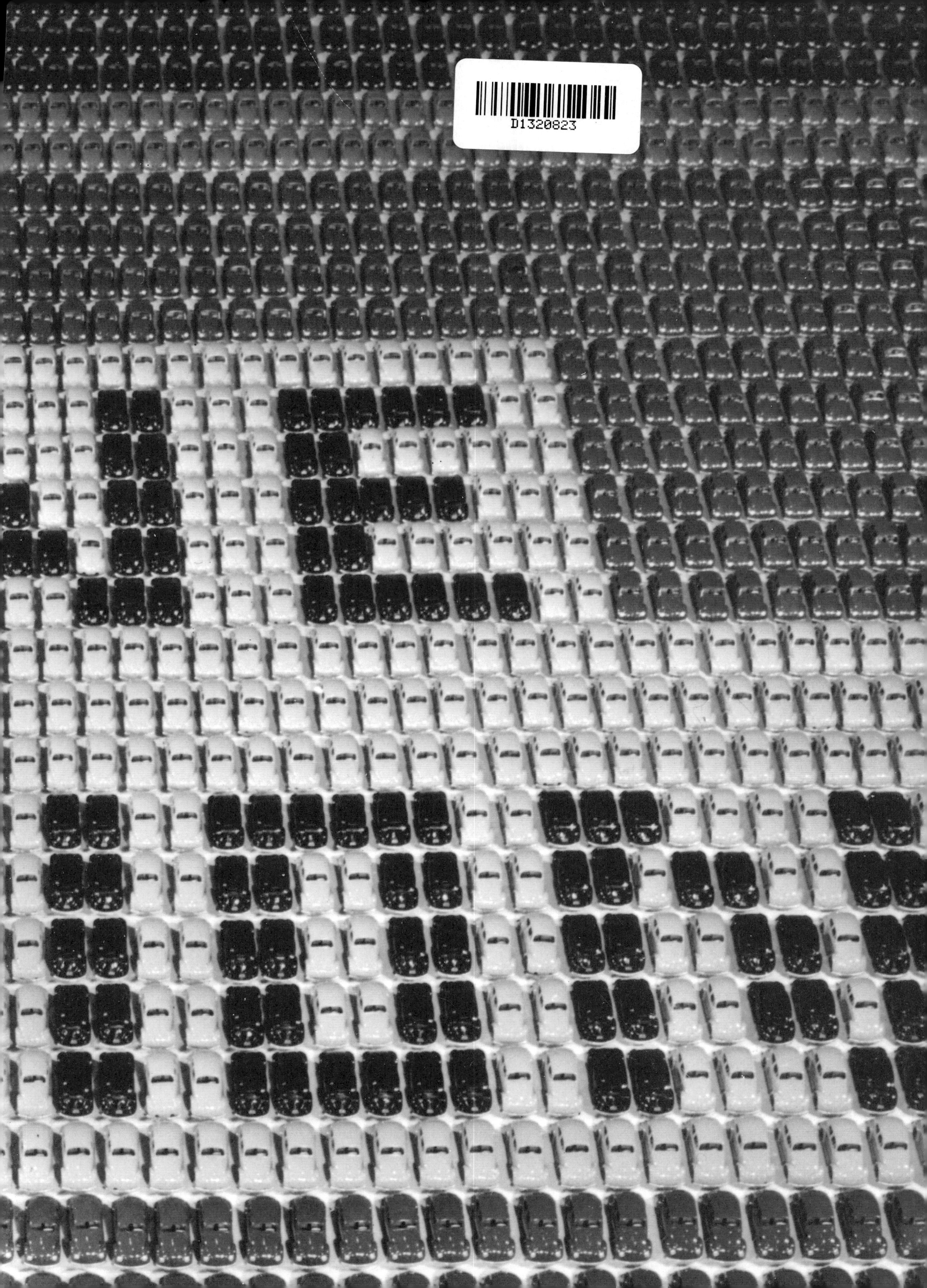

VW Beetle

VW Beetle

Clive Prew

Grange
BOOKS

Published by Grange Books
An imprint of Grange Books plc
The Grange
Grange Yard
London SE1 3AG

Produced by
Bison Books Ltd
Kimbolton House
117A Fulham Road
London SW3 6RL

ISBN 1-85627-034-3

Printed in Hong Kong

Reprinted 1993

Page 1: Though the shape, trim and mechanical make-up may have changed slightly over the years, the basic Beetle profile has remained remarkably faithful to Ferdinand Porsche's design.

Pages 2-3: It's the Käfer in Germany, the Maggiolino in Italy, the Fusca in Brazil and the Escarabajo in Spain. The French call it the Coccinelle, to the Dutch it's the Kever, but to most it's just the Beetle.

Below: Conceived and built by the Karmann company at Osnabrück, the four-seater Cabriolet was an essential part of the Volkswagen range from the earliest days of Beetle production.

Contents

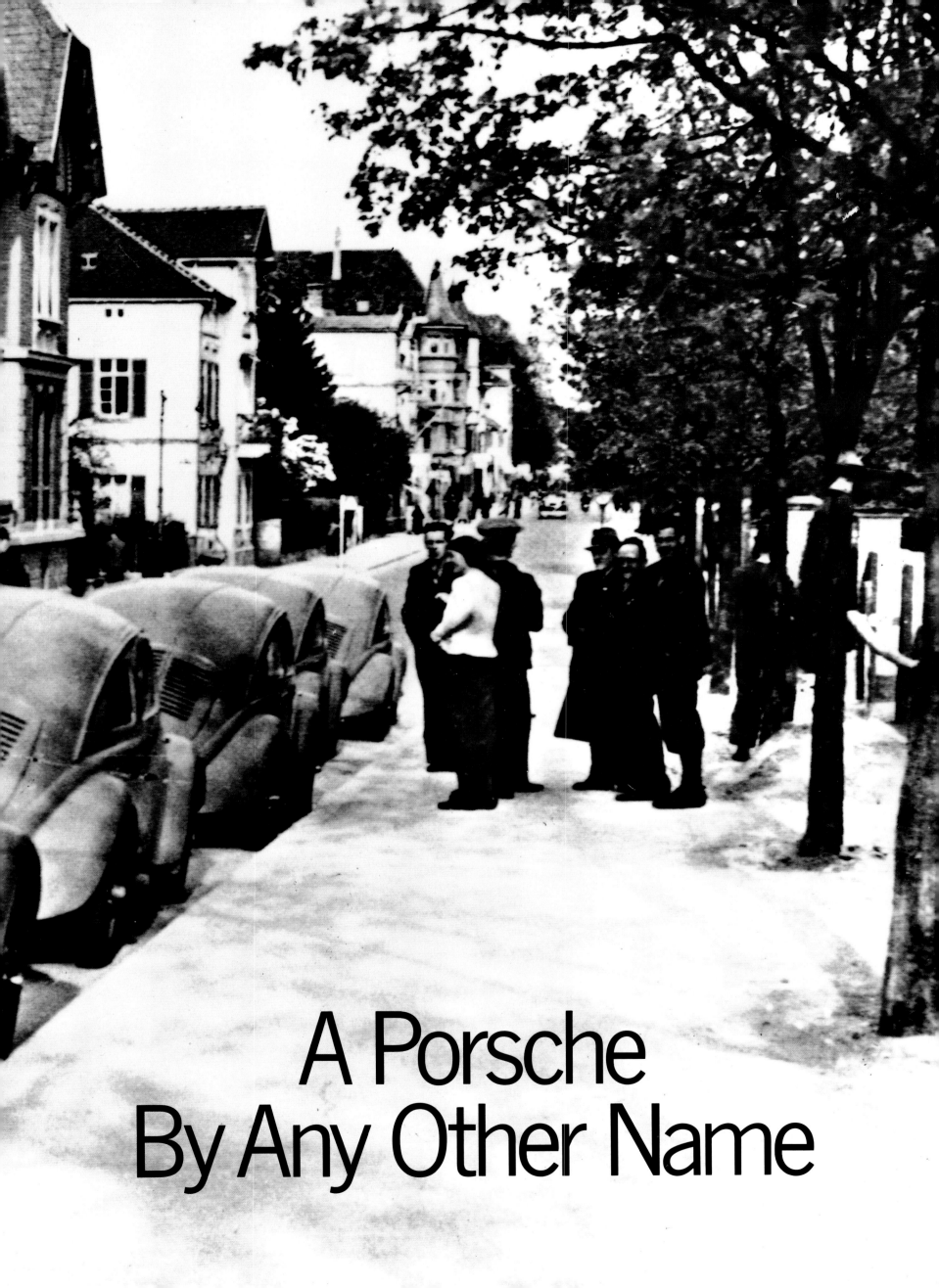

A Porsche
By Any Other Name

The Beetle story is also the story of Ferdinand Porsche. Without Porsche, there would have been no Volkswagen. So while it is not difficult to cite many others who have made lengthy and valuable contributions to the formation and continuation of the Volkswagen legend over the years, it is with the Porsche story that we must begin. Each of his early designs – their successes and failures – gave fascinating clues as to what would finally become the best selling car of all time.

Although the first production Beetles didn't hit the road until he was well into his sixties, Ferdinand Porsche was producing cars from quite an early age. And right from the start, there were indications that Porsche was not a man to follow the crowd when it came to automobile design.

Porsche was born in 1875, and produced his first blueprint in 1900. The Porsche-Lohner Chaise was powered by hub-mounted electric motors which drove the front wheels and apparently lasted for 50 miles before being recharged. The relatively new science of electricity was Porsche's first love so this route was no real surprise at the time. Later designs worked on what he termed the 'mixed fuel principle', using a small internal combustion engine which generated electricity to power the car, but eventually, he accepted more conventional drive methods.

As his career progressed, Porsche soon proved himself a hard worker and a designer of some genius. Here was a man who knew his own mind, though unfortunately, his ideas and plans for the automobile industry were not often shared by his employers. Having come from a working class background, his natural affiliations were less with the bosses and financiers as the workers. His first senior job, at Austro-Daimler, lasted 18 years and earned him eventual promotion to managing director, yet he resigned in 1923 after a boardroom row over cutbacks in the workforce. And when he went to the German Daimler company as technical director, another row caused a second resignation, though for different reasons.

Porsche harbored a desire to produce a cheap, affordable car for the masses – a car that everyone could own. He had designed that very thing at Daimler, codenamed Type 130 W01 and it had even reached the prototype stages. But a cheap car was the last thing the upmarket Daimler company wanted and it was this argument that led to his resignation, despite some brilliant work for the company including the awesome Mercedes SS and SSK models of the late 1920s. Notably, although the Type 130 W01 was front engined, it was designed with swing-axle rear suspension, something Porsche would come back to time and time again.

Fresh employment was not long in coming and the post of technical director with the Steyr company in Austria was his next appointment. He began on New Year's Day 1929 with a fresh enthusiasm, but the Wall Street Crash

aufgenommen April 1894 vor Abreise nach Wien

and its attendant far-reaching consequences led to a merger between Steyr and Daimler-Benz to create Steyr-Daimler-Puch. Porsche was suddenly back where he had been two years earlier. The new company immediately dropped his new projects and yet another resignation followed.

This time, however, he knew what to do. Although Ferdinand Porsche was now 55 years of age, he set up shop at 24 Kronenstrasse, Stuttgart in

Above: 1894. At the age of 19 Ferdinand Porsche installed this electricity generator system in his father's house.

Left: Porsche Number 1. The 1890 Porsche-Lohner Chaise, driven by two electric motors in the front hubs.

Right: After some frustrating rows with some of the large German manufacturers, Porsche set up his own business, partly in order to build a small, cheap car.

Previous pages: Meanwhile in a leafy suburb somewhere in Germany . . . The Beetle went through many changes before it reached production. And new prototypes were subjected to an exhaustive test program to prove the viability of the radical new design.

December 1930, forming his own design consultancy, Dr Ing hcF Porsche GmbH. Porsche was a man always destined to be his own boss; the only surprise was that it had taken him so long. To give his business the all-round technical expertise it needed, he made sure that certain key people were with him, people he had worked with and grown to respect during his long years in the motor industry. Under the new order, Porsche was to lay down the ideas and rough concepts, while the rest of the team filled in the details and made it work. His colleagues included Josef Kales, an air-cooled engine specialist; Karl Fröhlich, a transmission expert; Karl Rabe, who had been his chief engineer at Austro-Daimler; Josef Zahradnik for axle and steering design, and Josef Mickl, his aerodynamics advisor. Mickl at 45 was the oldest member of the team and Ferry Porsche, Ferdinand's son, was the youngest at 21. For a short time, there was also a business manager by the name of Adolf Rosenburger but as a Jew, he was forced to flee the country in 1933.

Although it was at this time that Porsche began to lay down the basic parameters for what would become the Volkswagen Beetle, it was very much an evolutionary design. Each subsequent attempt at the same concept produced a better car which was better engineered, more reliable and better looking than the last. To begin with, however, the Porsche consultancy were concerned with smaller matters – a crankshaft here, a rear axle there. One of their early triumphs was to patent 'Spring Suspension of Independent Car Wheels, especially for Motor Vehicles' – basically a torsion bar design, from which the Porsche company has drawn royalty payments ever since. It was not until 1931 that work began on the first of the Volkswagen prototype series, though the design was barely recognizable as a Beetle. The Beetle as we know it was still some 15 years away and even then the path towards it would be long and very winding.

With work slow in coming (at one point Porsche even borrowed on his life assurance to pay the men), the company had decided to produce some plans on a purely speculative basis. One of these projects was the Type 12, a small car suited to the economic depression. Fortunately, they quickly found a customer when Porsche went to see the Zündapp motorcycle company under Dr Fritz Neumayer, who wanted to diversify into the car market. Neumayer, however, insisted upon a five-cylinder water-cooled radial engine and because they needed the work, Porsche went along with it.

Despite this ludicrous engine choice, the design was still of some interest. Although it might have been considered unorthodox in terms of contempor-

ary schemes in the USA or Britain, it was not so odd compared to some of its European counterparts. A backbone chassis carried all-independent suspension with a transverse leaf spring at the front and a swing axle at the rear. The Type 12 had hydraulic brakes (incredibly, the Beetle 1200 Standard didn't get them until 1964) and all the controls ran through a central chassis member much as they would on the Beetle. There were other similarities too, mainly for weightsaving reasons. The rear-mounted engine meant no propshaft or torque tube.

Three prototypes – two sedans and one cabriolet - were built with bodies by Reutter. And for someone who had designed some of the most beautiful sports cars ever seen, this new design was definitely an odd one. The windshield was sharply raked, there were rear wheelarch spats, no running boards, and the back of the car arched right over in a giant arc. This was the birth of the Beetle shape.

Needless to say, the car was not a success. The engine overheated so severely that on one test, the engine oil actually boiled and welded the pistons to the cylinder walls. In the end, Neumayer's enthusiasm – and his money – ran out. 1932 quickly developed into a miserable year for Porsche. At one point, he seriously considered a 'blank cheque' offer to work in Moscow. But another small car opportunity was waiting round the corner.

Baron Fritz von Falkenhayn, head of the NSU plant at Neckarsulm, asked Porsche to design another light car suited to the prevailing hard times. What followed, the Type 32, was just that – and the next link in the Beetle story. Type 32 was also designed around a backbone chassis, but for the first time it was forked at the rear to carry the engine and transaxle arrangement. In addition, the front suspension used two of Porsche's patented torsion bars crossed transversely at the front with friction-type shock absorbers. The engine was a very Beetle-like oversquare 1470cc air-cooled flat four and was proved good for 75mph with no problems except excess noise. The bodies were designed by Erwin Komenda – still quite odd-looking but strangely futuristic for 1932, especially when compared with what Ford were producing in the early 1930s. Incredibly, one of the three original prototypes still survives in the VW museum, a steel-bodied version by the Drauz company of Heilbronn. The other two, by Reutter, another well-known coachbuilder, had fabric bodies with large, high-hinging trunk lids. Sadly, it was the steel-bodied car that caused the downfall of the whole project, simply because Fiat were also based at Heilbronn. Hearing about the new NSU car, Fiat reminded them of certain contractual obligations arising from their purchase of the old

NSU car factory. As part of the deal, NSU had agreed never to make cars under their own name again.

Once again Porsche was without a sponsor for the *Volksauto* (people's car) project. What it needed was a backer with a lot more cash, a lot more belief and a lot more vision. What it got was Adolf Hitler.

When Hitler took power communications were high on his list. There was the Volksradio project, which took his propaganda into every house in Germany; the Volksauto, to get the country mobile; and the giant autobahn program to make travel quicker and simpler for everyone (especially his troops).

How Hitler got to hear of Porsche's project was quite simple. An old friend from Daimler-Benz, Jakob Werlin, happened to call into the Porsche offices soon after NSU had pulled out, and was naturally told about the little Type 32. Werlin happened to be close to Hitler at this time and saw this as a way of earning favor with the Führer. So Hitler was told of the project and Porsche was driven to the Kaiserhof Hotel, Berlin to meet both Hitler and the Auto Union directors. Nazi propaganda also required that German cars dominate the race tracks in the mid-1930s and few people knew more about car design than Ferdinand Porsche, especially after his experience with the giant super-

Above left: One of the three Type 12s parked outside Porsche's house. This is one of the two sedans designed by Erwin Komenda and built by Reutter in 1932.

Above right: Although it was modified slightly in later years, this is the original 1934 Type 32 with steel body by the Drauz company of Heilbronn. Presumed lost, a German war veteran returned it to the factory in December 1950.

Right: The man without whom none of this would have been possible. Adolf Hitler accepts a convertible from Ferdinand Porsche.

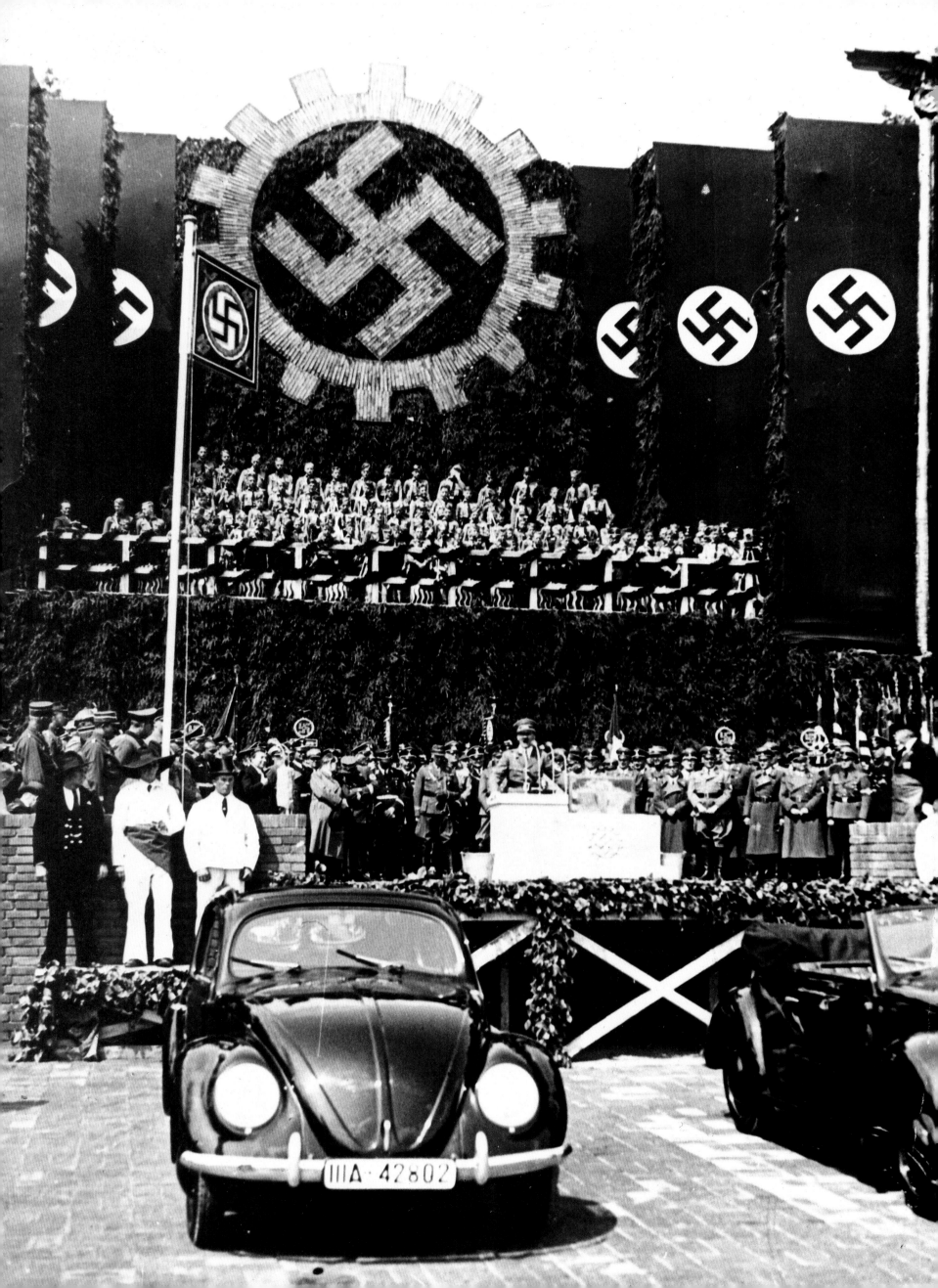

Left: Wolfsburg, 26 May 1938. Hitler dedicates the factory's cornerstone. Note stone masons in top hats and white overalls.

Right: Two Type 60 Volkswagens testing in the Black Forest, a sedan and a cabriolet with close-fitting side-screens. Used mainly for engine testing, these prototypes covered 50,000 miles over varied terrain.

Below: Ferdinand Porsche shows Hitler a Volkswagen sedan at the laying of the factory's foundation stone in 1938.

charged Mercedes. As it happened, Hitler knew quite a lot about cars himself, as is evidenced by some of his correspondence on the matter. He even gave Porsche some drawings of what he had in mind for the 'people's car', suggesting that it should be a four-seater family car with an air-cooled engine of one liter capacity. It should use only seven liters of gasoline per 100kms and be able to maintain 100km per hour.

Hitler persuaded the RDA (*Reichsverband der Deutschen Automobilindustrie,* the car manufacturers trade organization) to put Porsche under contract to develop the new state-financed car, even though they clearly saw it as a threat to their own business. Porsche was given around 233,000 Reichmarks to build the prototypes, but he was allowed only ten months not the full year he had requested, and his projected build-and-sell price of RM 1550 was slashed to a little over RM 900.

Designated Type 60, the new car carried many of the Type 32's features. Hitler had actually seen the plans himself by this time and even changed them a little, lowering the front hood contour to give it extra streamlining. After the allotted ten months, the cars were far from finished. The idea was that the other German car manufacturers would help Porsche produce the prototypes, but they didn't; jealousy still played a strong part in motor car design and manufacture. As the Porsche premises were only geared to design work, they built the cars in Porsche's own garage in Stuttgart. The only consolation was that at last they were building the car they wanted. They had the backing and the apparently unlimited funds of the state; and a very sympathetic client, even if he was Adolf Hitler . . .

By the end of 1935 they had two cars testing in the Black Forest, a sedan and a cabriolet. The design was a natural progression from the previous Types 12 and 32. Once again, the chassis was formed around a central backbone rounded at the top like the later Beetle, with a flat underside and wooden floorboards, which were later replaced by metal. It narrowed towards the front, where the central spine continued forward to clamp on to the twin torsion bars that formed the front suspension. The pedals sprouted out of the central spine just behind a small bulkhead and the battery tray was pressed into the rear of the pan under the back seat. The transmission was mounted on a cradle bolted between the two chassis forks and the engine hung off the back of the transmission. Rear suspension took the form of twin

Left: Curvy Type 30. Note fender-mounted headlights, limited access to under hood area and odd moulding which swoops from the nose of the car, around the screen pillars and over the roof.

Below: VW3-series cars had no rear window, but a row of giant louvers in the engine cover. Note how the doors hinge on the center pillar.

Right: Ferry Porsche at the wheel of the V2 cabriolet. In fact, the same car seen testing earlier. Note the rounded corners.

Below right: From the front, the VW3-series car has cutaway front fenders and square edges to the bonnet.

transverse torsion bars hidden in the rear crossmember with links to the rear hubs via a pair of thin blade-like radius arms. They had to be thin because they needed to flex for the suspension to work properly.

Engines were many and various. In fact with endless engine trials taking so long Porsche was granted a further 12 months development time. Each new design was designated a letter and it was E before they found one that did a good job at the right price. The A-Motor (a two-stroke) was rejected mainly because two-strokes didn't provide enough engine braking. The C-Motor was a sleeve-valved air-cooled twin and the D-Motor, designed by an engineer named Engelbrecht, was very like a noisy motorbike engine. Eventually they came up with the E-motor which by now was starting to look like a proper Beetle engine. The generator mount, front pulley, large heads, single wire mesh oil filter and distributor were all later Beetle engine features.

The body design was also evolutionary. The headlamps were mounted separately on the hood not on the fenders, it had vent windows and in line with Hitler's ideas for the car (he was financing it, after all), they lowered the hood line. The doors were of 'suicide' type – they hinged at the rear – but the most striking aspect of the car's design was its lack of rear window.

Two cars were built at first, a sedan (V1), coachbuilt by Reutter and a cabriolet (V2) by Drauz. But a further three were soon commissioned and designated VW3, the first of which was finished in early 1936 and again differed slightly. They were built by Daimler-Benz, indicating that other German manufacturers recognized that Hitler was not a man to be disobeyed.

Strangely the car featured many of the classic Beetle body mouldings curves and lines, but the hood and trunk cut right across them. The doors didn't open right down to the bottom of the body, either, leaving a strange sill effect and the fenders looked cut off at the ends, like some latter-day off-road racer. The hood opened from just below the screen line to a point about two-thirds down the nose, while at the rear the engine lid came right up the back of the car with a row of giant louvers.

It was that engine that stood out, though. A new member of staff, an Austrian designer by the name of Franz Reimspiess, joined the company in 1934 and almost immediately suggested a new four-cylinder engine every bit as cheap to produce as the two-cylinder design but producing far better results. A lightweight magnesium alloy crankcase, cast iron crank, overhead valves, aluminum cylinder heads and a very short camshaft with just four lobes to actuate the eight pushrods, were all aspects of the E-Motor's design.

By late 1936 the three VW3 prototypes were given to the RDA for extensive testing. They even re-engined the original V1 and V2 prototypes as further testbeds for the new engine. And the tests were strenuous, with two drivers covering over 400 miles a day over hills (the Alps), the Black Forest

and new autobahn stretches. The results were worth it though, as a total of 50,000 miles of testing proved what the design could and could not do. The cast-iron crankshaft was the biggest problem, as its repeated failure later led to the adoption of a forged steel unit. But other problems included broken shift levers and the electric fuel pump, which was soon swapped for a mechanical one. Despite reservations regarding the cable brakes and the front suspension design, the RDA's report, published at the end of 1937, gave Type 60 the go-ahead.

At the same time, Hitler decided that the whole project should be state funded through the German Labor Front (DAF), Hitler's state-run replacement for the banned trade unions. In reality however, this meant the German people themselves, as DAF funds comprised confiscated trade union funds and compulsory contributions of 1.5 percent of each worker's income. The Society for the Development of the German Volkswagen was formed in May 1937 and RM 500,000 was put forward for more prototypes.

The Series 30 (because 30 were built) cars were all put together by Daimler Benz. The front of the car was particularly Beetle-like with headlamps mounted on the front fenders and that characteristic hood line sloping right down to the nose of the car. Around the back, though, that unmistakable W shape that would become one of the early Beetle's most striking features, did not finish at the top of the engine cover, but continued over the roof, opening right out towards the corners of the front screen. The engine cover itself was now punched with massive louvers to give the engine as much cool

Left: A row of VW30s with their distinctive removable louvered engine lid and no rear window.

Below: The presentation drive to Berlin in 1939. By now the Beetle bodyshape was decided. And what an improvement on the prototypes! Note the fabric sunroof in the leading car.

Below right: Front and back covers of the original pay-as-you-earn KdF-Wagen brochure.

air as possible. Mechanically, the Series 30 cars followed the VW3. A change in compression ratio to 6:1 and a new oil cooler making up the engine modifications, while new split-leaf torsion bars at last stopped them snapping and depositing the car on the tarmac without the slightest warning.

If the VW3 was extensively tested, the Series 30 tests went to the limits of endurance. At an estimated cost of RM 30 million, 200 soldiers from the SS were drafted in to drive each car at least 50,000 miles over a variety of terrains. Ferry Porsche oversaw the operation.

All that was left was to finalize the styling. The job was given to Erwin Komenda and by 1938 the design was set. A few details were cleared up at this point, like making the door hinge in the right direction, changing the hood so that it hinged right at the top, and fitting bumpers and hubcaps for the first time, too. But it was the rear that saw the real modifications as they shortened the engine cover, introduced the famous 'pretzel' (because it looks vaguely like a German pretzel biscuit) or split rear window and fed the engine with air through a row of vertical louvers that sat beneath it. Forty-four of these new Series 38 cars were put together for further approval and testing.

When it came to ideas for actually getting Hitler's new car into production, the RDA began by suggesting various schemes, which said little except the fact that they weren't really interested. Their suggestion was that the existing German car manufacturers would share the burden of production, which would involve the government in a subsidy to the tune of RM 200 for each car. Hitler obviously worked out the cost of his projected production (a million cars a year) and decided that it would be cheaper to build his own factory instead.

Following the lead of most of the giant car plants of the time, the prime requirement was access to a navigable waterway. As the factory would literally take iron ore in one end and throw cars out at the other, they needed to be able to ship the raw materials and finished cars quickly and easily. It would even have its own power station, serving a new town as well as the factory. Hitler's choice was the village of Fallersleben on the banks of the Mittelland Canal. The site itself formed part of the 14th century estate of Schloss Wolfsburg, owned by Count von Schulenburg; needless to say, while he wasn't too happy about it, he had no chance of objecting to the plans himself and supporters were few and far between.

Like Ford's recently-built (1931) Dagenham plant in Britain, the Volkswagen factory would also have its own town where the workers would live. The car would be called the KdF-Wagen (*Kraft durch Freude* – Strength through Joy) and the town would be called KdF-Stadt. Officially, KdF was the leisure section of the DAF, its funds helping to finance bargain holidays for the workers, but in reality they were just misappropriated by the Nazis. Filled with the best American equipment and a large number of repatriated, US-trained workers, the major part of the factory was finished in early 1939. They needed the best of everything because right from the start, targets were high. Production was scheduled at 150,000 vehicles in 1940, building up to 1.5 million in two years. The car was available in only one color, a bluish grey and there was only one method of purchase.

In what was basically a system of financing production before any cars had to be handed over, German workers had to save up for their new KdF-Wagen by collecting special stamps. A minimum monthly payment of RM 5 would get a collecting card and there would be no sign of the car until the full RM 90 plus RM 50 delivery and another RM 200 for two year's insurance had been paid. (Average wages at this time were 200-300 RM per month.) No interest was paid on the investment and lost savings books could not be replaced. The agreement was non-cancelable, non-transferable and if you missed a payment, you lost the lot. Despite all these rather strict rules, some 336,688 people signed up for the scheme, either individually or in groups, raising RM 280 million.

Of course, not one of them ever got their car, as Hitler became preoccupied with more bellicose projects and invaded Poland on 1 September 1939. The Fallersleben factory went over to wartime production and after six years of fighting the KdF money was later seized by the Russians as war reparations.

Wartime Production

The factory that had promised so much, gave forth so little. Once Hitler had decided to extend Germany's borders, all vital resources were redirected to the war effort and the factory was still not complete by 1940.

The plant had been operational, but only just. By the time it moved over to wartime production, total KdF-Wagen production stood at 210 units but they had all gone to high-ranking Nazis. The first, redesignated Type 1, left the factory on 15 August 1940, and although production was kept up to provide much needed wartime transport, only 630 KdF-Wagens had been built by 1944. The factory was not idle, of course. In addition to cars, it was producing a host of other things including, at one time, 1.5 million primitive stoves for the German troops at the Russian front. Unfortunately, there were also V1 flying bombs and assorted parts for Junkers 88 bombers, which is why the factory itself was bombed by the Americans towards the end of the war.

The fact that the basic Beetle design had certain military possibilities had not escaped the army. In fact, one of the Series 30 chassis had been loaned to the army to have a gun and three seats fitted. It was hardly surprising then, that even before war had broken out, Porsche was asked to adapt the KdF-Wagen for use by the German army. In 1938, Franz Reimspiess designed a sort of cross-country vehicle, based on the KdF-Wagen floorpan with 19 inch wheels and not much at all in the way of bodywork. This rough design was rethought in 1939 and later after German tests at the very start of the war with Poland. The job of producing the Type 82 or Type 2, as it was labeled, was given to Ferry Porsche and the resulting car became known as the Kübelwagen or 'Bucket-car'.

The Kübelwagen went into production on 21 December 1940, but it was some time before the car was officially approved for use by the German army. By the end of that year, total production stood at 1000 and by the end of the war, around 50,000 had appeared from the Wolfsburg factory.

The Kübelwagen featured a KdF-Wagen-type chassis with the stock 985cc, 22.5hp engine and modifications for improved ground clearance. There was a change to the 1131cc, 25hp engine in March 1943. The bodies were supplied by Ambi-Budd in Berlin and the chassis were assembled in one area of the Wolfsburg plant. The simple ribbed body with its folding windshield and canvas top came with four doors, the front pair hinging at the back so they all swung off the same center pillar. Exterior features included two front towing hooks and twin fender-mounted headlamps with canvas covers, while a spade, black-out light and spare wheel were mounted right on top of the hood, which did not open and had no facility for storage, except for a five-gallon spare fuel can which slid into a specially tailored hole just above the pedal assembly. The proper fuel filler was just behind the spare wheel. Lastly, as the vehicle's lighting had to be geared to wartime, it included an ingenious rear light system with differing thicknesses of green plastic, enabling the driver to judge distance from the Kübelwagen in front by the number of lights that were visible.

The interior was no more than basic. In front were small individual bench seats that looked more like foldup picnic chairs covered in a lightly padded canvas. Rear seating took the form of a simple bench, and for added military discomfort, the air intake for the engine bay was right behind the rear seat, so quite what it sounded like with the top up and side curtains closed, one can only imagine.

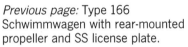

Previous page: Type 166 Schwimmwagen with rear-mounted propeller and SS license plate.

Above: Kübelwagens were assembled at the Wolfsburg plant with bodies from Ambi-Budd in Berlin.

Left: Kübelwagen with hood-mounted spare wheel, blackout driving lamp and shovel.

Right: Very early days at an almost deserted Wolfburg plant. Contrast this with picture on page 35.

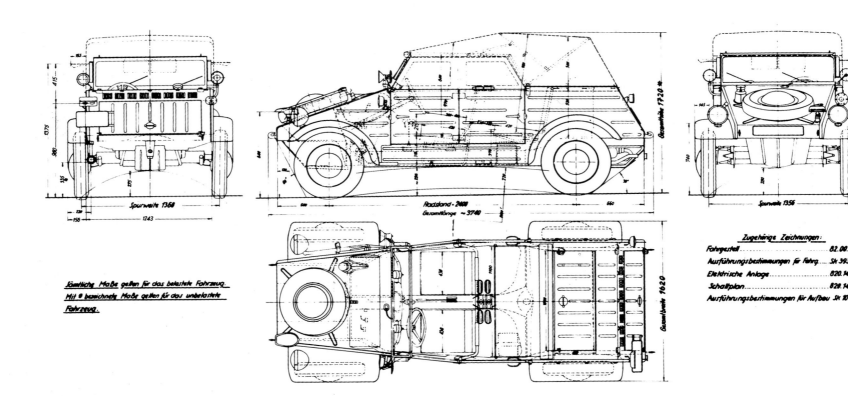

Sämtliche Maße gelten für das belastete Fahrzeug.
Mit ⊕ bezeichnete Maße gelten für das unbelastete
Fahrzeug.

Zugehörige Zeichnungen:

Fahrgestell 82.00.01
Ausführungsbestimmungen für Fahrg. ... Sk 3930
Elektrische Anlage 820.148.049
Schaltplan 820.140.090
Ausführungsbestimmungen für Aufbau Sk 10216

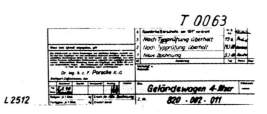

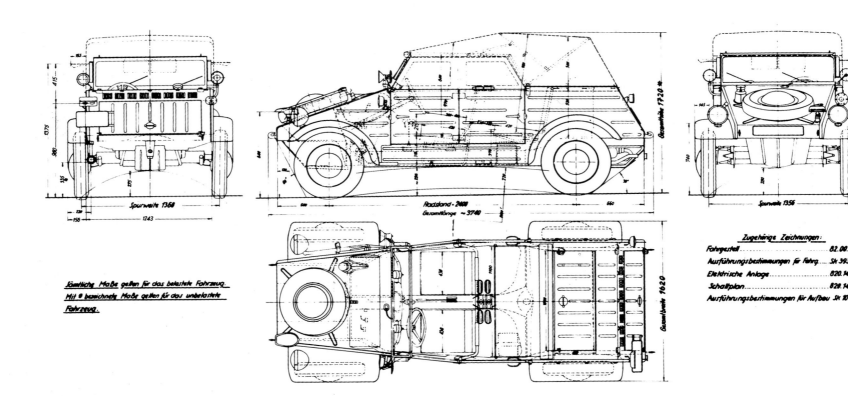

Left: Porsche plans for the Kübelwagen, dated 5 May, 1940.

Below left: From a total production of over 50,000, there are extremely few Kübelwagens left.

Right: The Schwimmwagen exhaust muffler was set high above the water level, but just behind passengers' ears.

Below: Whichever way you looked at it, the Schwimmwagen was never the most attractive of vehicles – really just a tub on wheels.

The improved ride height was achieved in the most ingenious manner. At the front, Porsche changed the design of the spindle slightly so that the wheel sat lower in relation to the two trailing arms. And at the back they used a reduction gear system at the end of each swingaxle, which had the added benefit of allowing the vehicle to drive at a walking (marching) pace. This reduction shift system resurfaced on the Volkswagen Microbus some years later.

With the many and varied tasks of military life, there was naturally more than one version of the Kübelwagen. Others included one that carried an air siren, one with a heavy-duty chassis and a dummy tank body for training purposes, a pickup version, a tropical delivery van, a snow caterpillar with half-tracks and one that was specially modified to run on railway tracks. There were even six four-wheel drive prototypes.

As the war continued and Rommel began to penetrate North Africa, they designed a special model for use in desert conditions with protected elec-

trics, extra cooling equipment and a larger air filter. Fortunately for the Allies, an organizational muddle sent these special Kübels to the Russian front while Rommel had to make do with ordinary ones, though they were at least equipped with special tyres.

Extra protection or not, the Kübelwagen with its rear-mounted air-cooled engine was a formidable desert performer. Captured German Kübelwagens were so popular with the Allied troops that the exchange rate became one Kübelwagen for two jeeps. And another story goes that a captured example, returned to Britain and dismantled for inspection, had 100lbs of sand removed from inside the bodyshell with the car still going strong.

If the Kübelwagen provided the German Army with basic everyday transport, the other high-volume wartime product from Wolfsburg did quite the opposite. Although it could easily trek across rough terrain, the fact that it was also amphibious was more than just a small bonus. In actual fact, the Schwimmwagen was so comfortable in the water that the Weapons Bureau seriously suggested that it should be fitted with colored navigation lights for port and starboard sides.

The Schwimmwagen was really just a sealed steel tub on wheels. There were obviously no doors but like the Kübelwagen, it came with a folding canvas top, blackout light and hood-mounted spare wheel. Apart from a few added exterior trappings like a paddle and a spade, the main giveaway, was the externally mounted propeller, hinged just below the engine lid. The propeller was raised and lifted with a detachable rod that extended right over the back of the car. It was stored above the exhaust muffler, which was high above the water level but also just behind the rear passengers' ears. The louvered engine cover incorporated a cutout for the propeller when it was in the raised position, and once lowered, it located automatically in a three-dog spline fitting, driven by the crankshaft. The engine air intake was obviously high out of the water but right below the muffler, so quite how it performed with a constant supply of nice hot air is another matter.

Like the Kübelwagen, the Schwimmwagen came in a number of different configurations. The earliest version, the Type 128 began with the 984cc engine, but later versions all came with the bigger 1131cc engine (increased bore by 5mm to 75mm), 25hp engine. The German Waffenamt (the weapons department) had set 25hp as the basic minimum military requirement. The Type 138 followed and eventually the Type 166, the most sophisticated

model, with a shorter wheelbase and low weight, which was soon regarded as the hot rod Schwimmwagen, most of them going straight to the SS.

Not only could these cars swim, but they also came with four-wheel drive. The transmission was interesting in that it worked normally in two-wheel drive until fifth gear was engaged, though some brought in four-wheel drive with a second small lever behind the gear shift. It is interesting to note that Kübelwagens had two fuel tanks with fillers in the hood plus another filler for the front axle pressure lubrication system (to overcome water immersion). Going flat out, the Schwimmwagen was good for 50mph on dry land and just over 6mph in water. That the Schwimmwagen was, indeed, waterproof was proved on many occasions by British officers at Wolfsburg after the war. Apparently, the practice was to drive the Schwimmwagen off the landing wharf straight into the Mittleland Canal at 40mph. The car would bellyflop into the water, bob about on the surface and cruise back to the jetty.

In the end, some 14,238 Schwimmwagens were built both at the Wolfsburg factory and at Porsche's small facility (they had moved by now to a new premises with workshops) in Stuttgart before the end in 1944.

Kübel and Schwimmwagens were not the only wartime Wolfsburg products, of course. Throughout the war, Porsche and his design team were busy producing designs for all sorts of military hardware. Others include the Type 82E, the Type 92 Kommandeurwagen and the Type 87 Leichte Kavallerie model, all of which combined the Beetlish body of the KdF-Wagen with one of the Kübel's high-riding chassis. The Type 87 was probably the most interesting as it used an experimental four-wheel drive Kübelwagen chassis. Quite a number were built, as production totalled 134 in 1942, 382 in 1943, 151 in 1944 and just two (presumably from left over parts) in 1946. These last two even incorporated a roller at the nose to help them over lumps in the ground.

Above left: With its shorter wheelbase and lower weight, the Type 166 was the final and ultimate Schwimmwagen.

Left: The rear-mounted propeller located automatically into a spline-fitting and took its drive straight from the crankshaft.

Above: As if proof were needed – a Schwimmwagen doing what it was made for. Note the rod at the back for pulling the propeller back into place.

Right: Schwimmwagens were never noted for their interior luxury. Note the curious pedal arrangement with accelerator on the left.

Left: Beetle in wartime clothing with headlamps almost totally covered, and high ride-height suggesting a Kübelwagen chassis.

Below: No, not the real thing, but a model built to show the extent of the bomb damage to the Wolfsburg factory.

Right: The somewhat boxy Type 83 van, built for the German Post Office. There was also an ambulance version.

Below right: Incredibly, the damage sustained by the Wolfsburg factory at the hands of the US Air Force still didn't stop production.

From April until August 1944, the Volkswagenwerk was subjected to a number of daylight air raids by US bombers. A mystery pilotless British bomber crashed into the plant on 29 April, but it is presumed that it was pure chance that it hit the factory at all. By the end of the war, attacks had totally flattened a large part of the plant. Floor area rendered totally unusable amounted to 33.8 percent, over 20 percent of the machinery was wrecked and a large part of the roof was brought down, rendering what was underneath virtually useless too. Although the company claimed that only 60 percent of the factory was destroyed, what was left was hardly the basis for the production of anything, let alone cars. Production was revived, but output was slow at only a quarter of the previous average and did not last for very long either.

The plant at Fallersleben and its slave-labor force were liberated by the American army on 10-11 April 1945. (Officially the actual plant and town were never liberated because they were too new to be on their maps.) Knowing that the US army were close, however, the guards fled, leaving the workers, most of them foreign prisoners of war, to run riot. They wrecked most of the machinery and burned nearly all the records. Fortunately the Germans had taken the precaution of packing many of the key machinery parts in crates and stowing them in electrical conduit pipes under the factory floor. These would prove invaluable to the British who were to take over the plant and the administration of its remaining staff. Partly because they had nowhere else to go, and partly because the British at least had a little food to offer, some workers stayed on and another 522 Kübelwagens were produced between August and December that year. The war was over, but the problems at Wolfsburg had hardly begun.

The British Years

By the end of the war, Porsche's dream must have looked less likely than ever. The postwar division of Germany into individual political zones had placed the Fallersleben factory under British control, but there still remained the question of what to do with it. Six successful bombing raids had left the factory all but wrecked and what machinery they had left was beginning to rust away. The whole place was inches deep in water too, since there was no roof on most of the factory. Added to this, there were few staff and very little accommodation for them anyway, so the immediate call for the place to be pulled down and rebuilt elsewhere is understandable. An unexploded bomb nearly settled the factory's fate: found wedged between the two main generators of the power station, had it exploded, there is no doubt that it would have meant the final dismantling of the Wolfsburg plant and certainly no more Volkswagen cars. The fact that the factory picked itself up and got back to work was not so much through any grand plan, but more likely because there was nothing else to do.

When the British took over from the Americans in the early summer of 1945, they were quick to take advantage of what resources there were by installing a REME (Royal Electrical and Mechanical Engineers) maintenance and repair shop in one part of the factory buildings. They renamed it the 'Wolfsburg Motor Works', and the few German workers that remained at the plant began to fix the machinery back together and even managed to produce two complete cars from the one surviving sheet metal press. One of these first postwar cars was immediately despatched to the local British Army headquarters and incredibly, solicited an order for more. To Major Ivan Hirst, the plant's commanding officer, this was tacit approval of the job they had managed to do at Wolfsburg (by now the first town council had renamed

the town too) and he took it as the go-ahead to make the plant operational as soon as possible.

With typical military efficiency, the first thing the British did was to introduce a model number system to correctly identify the assorted models. The old KdF-Wagen was the Type 1, the Kübelwagen was Type 2, and the Kübel chassis with the KdF-Wagen sedan body was the Type 5. In addition, there was a second digit which identified the actual body type: sedan was 1, convertible was 5 and so on. The final list included a Kübelwagen fire tender, assorted delivery vans and both open and closed trailers.

It may have been comprehensive, but it was also wishful thinking at the time, because with no parts or raw material, finished cars were a rarity. Production did build up for a while in June, July and August as they used up what remaining parts they had. For a short time, they were still supplied with Kübelwagen bodies from Ambi-Budd in Berlin, but this ceased once Berlin became part of the Russian sector. Actual production figures read 138 Kübelwagens in June 1945, increasing to 235 in July and another 136 in August. By September though, parts were probably used up, as only 11 made it out of the factory that month; in December total Kübelwagen production had fallen to one a month, and in February 1946, the last example left the plant.

There was much more to do than just build cars, though. In 1945, the whole area was filling up with refugees from the East, most of whom were fleeing the Russian sector (what would eventually become East Germany). By the end of 1945 there were around 6000 workers at Wolfsburg, half engaged in the manufacture of what vehicles they could, the rest just clearing up the mess, attempting to patch some temporary covering over the roof

Previous page: With the plant still in ruins, postwar production began in 1945, though most of the first Beetles were actually built on a Kübelwagen chassis, standing three inches higher than the standard sedan.

Below left: The sign that says it all: 'No. 2 REME, Auxiliary Workshops'. The British had arrived.

Right: Pre-empting the later Hebmüller cabriolet by two years, Colonel Charles Radclyffe had this one-off twin-carburetored cabriolet built for himself in 1948.

Below right: Earliest dashboard with twin glove boxes and gearshift layout.

and generally just trying to turn a mile long pile of rubble into a car plant. While so many workers was obviously a good thing, their sheer numbers brought further problems. Food and decent living accommodation were every bit as rare in Germany as raw materials for the plant. British army trucks brought coal for the generators, but because the rest of Europe was experiencing exactly the same problem, the only way to get what was wanted was to barter for it. Most of the time, they were building cars just to trade for the materials to build more cars. It didn't matter who eventually got the car – in fact, most of the dealing was illegal anyway – it was simply the act of getting enough steel or even the simple things like light bulbs that mattered. At the time it was reckoned that one new car could get you one week's supply of steel.

Production wasn't limited to the Kübelwagen either. Using the old KdF sedan body on the Kübelwagen chassis, the Type 51 started to appear in August 1945, presumably as the supply of Kübelwagen bodies dried up. By the end of that first year, as many as 703 Type 51s had been built along with 713 Type 93 closed trailers, 275 Type 83 sedan-based closed delivery vans and 219 Type 28 Kübelwagen-based closed deliveries. When it came to the ordinary Type 11 saloons, only 58 appeared that year, most of them built in December.

Setting the style for a further 16 million Beetles, those first, lonely few came with some very interesting features. For a start there were no vent windows; in fact they didn't appear until October 1952 on the Export model. At the rear, there was still the famous 'pretzel' split rear window with the large vertical air vents beneath it, while the rear engine cover featured that classic W-shaped moulding and a small combined stop and license plate light. The rear lights, which were to undergo many a change over the Beetle's 35 year history, began as tiny round units to fit the curvature of the rear fenders.

Compared with the cars of even a year or two later, the earliest Beetles came with very little in the way of interior comfort. Simple plain wool cloth-covered seats were lightly padded with horsehair, while the hardboard door panels were covered in leathercloth. A spindly black three-spoke steering wheel with its central horn button sat in front of the simplest of dashboards. It comprised two central panels in relief, one housing the speedometer, the other just embossed with the circular VW logo. Optimistically reading to 120km per hour, the speedo had the ignition switch directly beneath it and two nicely shaped knobs either side. A further knob, in the center of the dash

worked the semaphore turn signals. Even at these early stages, the car came with heating, piped through a single heat exchanger on the back of one of the exhaust pipes to a single outlet in the front bulkhead on the driver's side. At the time, Volkswagens were available only in a blue/gray, the original non-committal KdF color. There were special colors for the military however. The British Army had some in green, the Coal Board had black, the RAF and US Army sedans were gray and the Russians were allowed a few in maroon.

Those Russian cars count as among the first exported Volkswagens, the only others being the few that were taken home by foreign servicemen and a trainload commandeered by the French in 1946. Apparently the British had to entertain Soviet officers while their 50 drivers were taught to drive outside!

There was no chromework on those early cars so the bumpers with their little overriders were usually black. The 'nipple type' hubcaps (the center bulge to clear the hub center nut) were also painted.

On the mechanical side, the first Beetles used the 1131cc motor from the wartime Schwimmwagen. From a bore and stroke of 75 and 64mm and a

Above: Going by the uniforms, this could be the trainload of early Beetles commandeered by the French in 1946.

Left: By 1948 Beetles had swapped their 'nipple' hubcaps for domed caps with a large VW emblem. By 1949 the hood was no longer secured with a small locking handle.

Right: By the end of 1946, production had really picked up. This was the 10,000th car, seen on 14 October with workers' placard complaining about lack of food.

compression ratio of 5.8:1, the flat four developed 25 hp at 3300rpm. It was built around a two-piece crankcase with bolt-on finned barrels and a centrally mounted camshaft, gear driven directly off the forged steel crankshaft, which sat above it. The pushrods ran in separate tubes to the aluminium alloy heads. The distributor was also driven off a gear on the end of the crankshaft, while the generator was mounted on a pedestal, cast-in as part of the crankcase. The other end of the generator was connected to the all-important upright engine cooling fan.

The very earliest KdF-Wagens came with a cylindrical fuel tank under the bonnet, but this was soon changed for an 8-gallon rectangular version. The reserve fuel lever, hidden away in the passenger footwell (it was later centralised) allowed access to the last gallon of gasoline through an ingenious dual-level tap device at the bottom of the tank. Gasoline was supplied to the engine through a mechanical fuel pump into a small carburettor, which until the war had always been a downdraft Solex, but as Solex were in Berlin (the Russian sector) after the war, they lost supply until April 1950. The home-built unit comprised a body and float chamber made at the factory from die-cast aluminium, with the smaller parts coming from the German camera makers, Voigtlander. Exhaust gases exited from both ends of each cylinder head into a small single exit exhaust muffler, mounted just under the rear valance. The driver's side (left-hand drive) exhaust had the small heat exchanger for the heating system, of course. And as the very early cars had little or no sound insulation around the engine bay, they were exceedingly noisy.

In the suspension department, things were still very simple. At the front, two transverse tubes carried split-leaf torsion bars. Five leaves in the upper tube, four in the lower. These were fixed in the center of the tubes with a pinchbolt and connected to the four rearward pointing trailing arms. And these in turn were fixed to the spindles and spindle arms via linkpins and traditional kingpins. Single-acting shock absorbers all round were by Hemscheid. And steering was a simple worm and nut box, connected to the steering wheel via a flexible 'doughnut'.

At the rear, following the Type 60 design, the four-speed transmission conveyed the drive via two swing axles, held in place at the rear hubs by single blade-like control arms which connected them to the transverse torsion bars.

Car production aside, the long running debate over who should actually own the factory and the facilities it offered continued throughout 1945. Technically, the Wolfsburg facility was on offer to the Allies as part of the war reparations, yet on repeated occasions no other country took up the offer. This was partly because a half-demolished factory and a few battle-scarred machines was hardly the most desirable of prizes, but also because the chauvinistic British motor industry refused to see the value of Porsche's basic design.

Because the military had found the little car so very effective during the war, one of the very first post war Beetles was sent to England for appraisal. The bastions of the British car industry did not share the Army's enthusiasm, finding the car too ugly, noisy and generally too odd. Compared with what was on offer in Britain in the immediate post war period, the Beetle was completely incongruous, so their reaction is understandable. Later that year, a delegation from the British Society of Motor Manufacturers and Traders (SMMT) visited the factory and wrote a report, 'Investigation of the Developments in the German Automobile during the Post War Period'. This was followed by a further report, published in 1946. Entitled, 'Investigation into the Design and Performance of the Volkswagen or German People's Car', it contained a comparative road test between a Hillman Minx Mk III and the Volkswagen that had been sent to England some months earlier. No doubt on the say-so of the few engineers at the Humber car company who had evaluated the Volkswagen, the British eventually turned both car and factory down. And although this was proved very bad judgement, they can take comfort in the fact the they were by no means the only ones.

In February 1947 the Australian Reparations Commission turned down the chance, and in February 1948 Henry Ford II did the same. At a well-documented meeting in Cologne in March 1948, Mr Ernest Breech, one of Ford's advisors summed it up with the words, 'I don't think what we're being offered here is worth a damn'. One wonders what his thoughts were 20 years later when Volkswagen became Germany's biggest company and Volkswagen vehicles were being built at a rate of one every eight seconds and exported to 130 countries across the world.

The only country who did express an interest was Russia, who approached the British authorities in the summer of 1948. Unfortunately for them, East-West relations had already begun to cool and plans were in hand to give it

back to the West Germans, so the bid was rejected, along with another idea which would have moved the Soviet border so as to place the plant just inside the Russian sector.

Despite the various rejections, it wasn't until 1949 that the plant was finally returned to the Germans. It was only through the ingenuity and sheer stubbornness of the British officers in charge of the plant that Wolfsburg survived the immediate postwar upheaval at all. Major Ivan Hirst had secured an order for 10,000 Volkswagens in 1946 and production was growing all the time. But struggle was very much the order of the day. Using the traditional, though frowned upon, method of bartering for the things they needed, whole trainloads of coal were diverted to Wolfsburg, and much needed machinery was mysteriously 'acquired' from other parts of the country. The plant was steadily turned from a bomb site into a proper functional car factory, although production stopped if it rained.

Production grew to about 1000 cars a month in 1946 for a yearly total of 7767 vehicles. There were a few Type 51s, the odd Type 93 trailer and one Kübelwagen but for the most part, the factory mainly turned out the plain old Type 11 sedans. The total for 1947 was up slightly at 8987 vehicles, but the problems of supply were still huge and what was produced was still only available to certain people. And 'certain people' didn't include the general public.

Just as the many pre-production Volkswagens had been a gradual evolutionary movement towards a more advanced and generally better specification, so the production models now began to change almost imperceptibly for the better. The 'nipple hubcaps', for example were altered slightly to take in the larger VW badge in the center with lettering in black if the car was black but red for any other exterior color. This was also the first year of the new 'pope's nose' rear stop and license plate light.

On 1 January 1948, Volkswagen gained a new general manager. Appointed by Major Hirst and his immediate superior Colonel Charles Radclyffe, on the recommendation of the German Association of Automobile Manufacturers, Heinrich (Heinz) Nordhoff was the man who would carry the company through the next 20 years of development and incredible growth.

Nordhoff was 49 years old when he came to Volkswagen, and although he had found himself homeless and penniless after the war, his prewar experience at both BMW and Opel stood him in good stead. When the war ended Nordhoff was saved, literally by hours, from returning to Berlin where he would have been captured with the other Opel executives and sent to Russia, where they were never seen again. Instead, he was running a tiny Opel repair shop in Hamburg when he was contacted by Radclyffe. When he took over at Wolfsburg, he had never driven a Volkswagen and certainly had no immediate relish for the conditions that confronted him.

His first job was to inform the existing German chief executive, Dr Hermann Münch, that his services were no longer required. Although it took several phone calls to Radclyffe before Münch believed what was happening, Nordhoff later called it 'one of the most painful episodes of my life'. Never-theless, Nordhoff was Wolfsburg's 'new broom' and Radclyffe had agreed that the British would not interfere. Problems did not disappear overnight, but one of his employees later said that Nordhoff gave the company direction. Before his arrival, the Wolfsburg Motor Works had been in a rut, short of both food and vital manufacturing materials; Nordhoff somehow changed the atmosphere by making his presence felt. He provided the company with strong leadership and quietly, but firmly, got everything moving.

To indicate in no uncertain terms that he was now in charge, he began by removing two of the signs outside the factory. The 'Wolfsburg Motor Works' sign, was replaced by the German 'Volkswagenwerk', and another in the car park which announced, 'For British Officers Only' was removed for good. He also formalized the production, personnel and finance departments and even a public relations department, headed by Frank Novotny, later one of the company's chief directors.

Despite stumbling from one crisis to another (mainly the cash problems of paying the workers, but also bad living conditions and pressures to scrap the whole design), Nordhoff and his workforce managed to produce 19,244 Beetles that year – all the more incredible when you consider that many assembly line workers were standing up to their ankles in water every time it rained and that they had to light fires near many machines to keep the hydraulic fluid from freezing. Most importantly, the percentage of these cars going to the occupying forces was drastically reduced. From September to November 1948, only 300 Beetles went to the Forces and 2154 were built in October alone. Of these, some were exported, leaving 1270 that were sold to the German public. The waiting list, however, amounted to some 15,000 cars at home and another 7000 abroad.

All factory repairs and new equipment had to be paid for through hard-earned sales revenue so progress was inevitably slow. The cars were not of the highest quality either. The paint was bad, the engines didn't last long and the suspension, although it worked, needed serious refinement. At first, anyone achieving over 100,00kms in a Volkswagen received a personal letter of congratulation and a gold watch from the factory, though this practice was soon withdrawn as the cars became more reliable.

With postwar demand for cars so strong, Nordhoff had no worries about increasing production to an absolute maximum. In the first six months of 1949, production was almost tripled, and in May the 50,000th postwar Volkswagen was celebrated with a special dinner (real coffee!) in the works canteens. As a reminder of the appalling conditions, however, it was noted that in some areas, the cooks still had to work under umbrellas, as the rain poured in through the roof. By the end of the year they'd managed 46,154 vehicles (including 8 of the new Transporter delivery vans), a tally that counted for 50 percent of Germany's total automotive production. Daily production amounted to an average 185 vehicles.

So it was on 6 September that the factory was handed back to the Germans. The ownerless *Volkswagenwerk GmbH (Gesellschaft mit beschrankter Haftung*, a company with limited liability) finally became the property of the

Left: Early development and testing at the Porsche workshops in Zuffenhausen. Ferdinand and Ferry Porsche are both in hats, while Hans Klauser, long time Porsche employee, looks on.

Right: In later years, Dr Heinrich Nordhoff with one or two staff outside the Wolfsburg plant.

German Federal Republic under the guidance of the State of Lower Saxony.

It is a sad footnote to the pioneering spirit of the Volkswagenwerk that Professor Ferdinand Porsche himself had no involvement in the rebirth of the plant and indeed probably knew very little of what was going on there. From mid-1945 onwards, his treatment at the hands of successive governments can only be understood in the light of the whole postwar attitude towards suspected Nazis and the German people in general.

It seemed to the Allies that Porsche had done rather too much for Hitler; not only had he made 'the People's Car', but his factory had produced military material too. Porsche underwent intensive questioning, first by the British and then by the American forces. Now 70, he spent three months imprisoned with Albert Speer in a castle outside Stuttgart, before being released and allowed to settle in Zell am See, near his workshop in Gmünd, Austria. On the journey, he tried to visit his old offices in Stuttgart, now occupied by the Americans but was not allowed past the gate.

Unfortunately the worst was yet to come. Later, Porsche was invited to Germany to speak to the French about 'an interesting assignment'. Assuming that the Wolfsburg plant was now doomed, he listened with interest to the French plans to build their own version of the Volkswagen. They even claimed that they had been given the Wolfsburg plant and were having it shipped to French soil. The reality was something quite different. That weekend Porsche was arrested along with others in his party. It seems that rival

French car manufacturers, having heard of the pending scheme, had arranged for Porsche to be interned for alleged violations of the Hague Convention. The charges were totally misguided, and this was proved two years later when he was completely exonerated, but by then the damage had been done. Imprisoned in Baden-Baden and later in an unheated dungeon in Dijon, Porsche's health declined.

In another episode, this time involving Ghislaine Kaes, Porsche's nephew and secretary for most of his working life, the French forced him to surrender the Volkswagen blueprints. Although they failed to get the blueprints, they did receive bail amounting to a million French francs, half a million each for Porsche and Dr Anton Piëch, his son-in-law, which was paid by Ferry Porsche who earned the money designing a racing car for Cisitalia, the Italian company. Ferdinand Porsche had by then spent almost two years in prison for his forced association with the Nazis.

Porsche did eventually witness the Wolfsburg miracle, visiting the plant in September 1950, and spending the day discussing the company's future with Dr Nordhoff and assorted other company personnel. It is reported that on his return home Porsche was overcome almost to tears, noting the autobahns stocked full of Beetles, the car that he had fought for so long to develop and promote. The French finally acquitted him, though they never returned his half million francs, and Ferdinand Porsche, the father of the Volkswagen Beetle, finally died on 30 January 1951.

Excellence & Exports

The fact that Volkswagenwerk Gmbh was now safe in German hands had little effect on Nordhoff's plans. He knew where the company was going from day one and the matter of who actually owned the plant, was of little consequence.

The master plan depended on certain fixed decisions about what the company should do and be. The first was that they should pursue a one-model policy, much as Henry Ford had done with his Model T. True, there were variations on the theme, but the basic design philosophy that ran through the whole range was one of unity of design ideas. Although the introduction of the Type 2 van and the Type 3 and 4 passenger cars later proved this policy both hasty and commercially unviable, all those models shared much the same suspension and engine design principles, so they did at least retain the Volkswagen family likeness. Another decision was that the basic Beetle body shape should remain the same, despite strong pressures, especially from export markets to change it. Modifications to the Volkswagen would be evolutionary, gradual and always only with good cause. Improved quality was very much an immediate priority, however, and something Nordhoff addressed with continual vigor. A third policy was to open up new markets throughout the world, partly by creating a special upmarket export version of the basic German Beetle.

The home market was beginning to flourish by this time. Dr Karl Feuereissen, Nordhoff's sales and marketing genius, had set up over 200 Volkswagen dealerships with another 200 service and repair shops throughout West Germany. But it was the Export models that would lead the way to smarter, better equipped Volkswagens, far removed from those spartan early models.

The first Export model was launched on 1 July 1949 and along with the introduction of two new Volkswagen Cabriolets, the Karmann 4-seater and Hebmüller 2-seater versions (of which, more later), heralded yet more changes to the Volkswagen model numbering system. After a shortlived system which used suffix letters to denote export or home market, right or left hand drive models, with extra letters for the optional sunroof, the new model numbers read as follows:

Type 101: Standard left-hand drive chassis
Type 102: Standard right-hand drive chassis
Type 111: Standard left-hand drive sedan

LIMOUSINE

STANDARD- UND EXPORT-MODELL

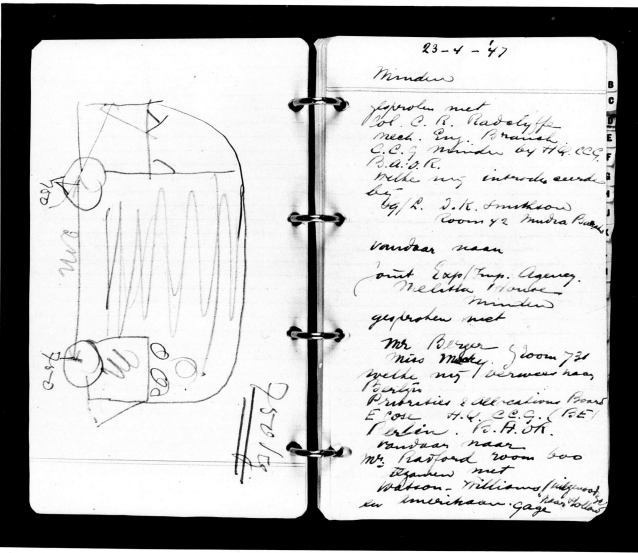

Previous pages: One of the first British imports. The 'Colborne-Baber' Beetle.

Above: Early Volkswagen promotional material used heavily stylized drawings to make the car look even better. Limousine meant sedan.

Left: Porsche's 1947 notebook showing first plans for a Volkswagen van. Note the two meter wheelbase and weight distribution calculations.

Right: Early Export Beetles. Note the split rear windows, 'Pope's Nose' rear license plate light and chrome trim.

Type 112: Standard right-hand drive sedan
Type 115: Standard left-hand drive sedan with sunroof
Type 116: Standard right-hand drive sedan with sunroof
Type 103: Export left-hand drive chassis
Type 104: Export right-hand drive chassis
Type 113: Export left-hand drive sedan
Type 114: Export right-hand drive sedan
Type 117: Export left-hand drive sedan with steel sunroof
Type 118: Export right-hand drive sedan with steel sunroof
Type 151: Karmann left-hand drive Cabriolet
Type 152: Karmann right-hand drive Cabriolet

The Hebmüller two-seater Cabriolet (left-hand drive only) was originally numbered 14A, and was never renumbered, presumably because production was only brief.

With the new model numbers came more improvements for the 1949 model year. The Volkswagen model year, incidentally, ran from January to December until 1955. The 1956 model year began on 1 August 1955 and subsequent years always ran from August to August. So dates quoted here for changes in the car's equipment or construction refer to model years, not the strict calendar dates. It must also be remembered that changes introduced in Germany may not correspond immediately with those in other countries. New in 1949 was a cable-release hood catch to replace the previous locking external handle, while at the back, the manual engine starting handle and its bumper-mounted support bracket were finally discontinued. Presumably, Nordhoff had enough faith in his electric starter by this time. There was also a change in the floorpan about this time which gave rear passengers proper footwells.

Volkswagen engines didn't have the best reputation for reliability and long service, and 1949 saw the first steps to improve on both. In June, better crankcase breathing was introduced, while in September the metal composition of the cylinders was altered to increase the amount of phosphorus for longer engine life. Magnesium replaced aluminum for the transmission case to make it even lighter. The chassis did not escape modification either, and the Beetle gained improved roadholding with new double-acting shock absorbers, soon followed by an extra leaf in the bottom torsion bar in 1950.

As was the intention, the Export models meant quite an improvement in both the quality and the level of equipment. Nordhoff knew that the only way to build sales was to export, and he knew that those cars had to be good right from the start. There was even a range of proper colors and some chrome trim — luxuries previously unheard of for Beetles.

Above: Looking more like a hood, this is actually the engine cover of the rare two-seater Hebmüller cabriolet.

Left: 1949 marked the first year of the Export model with chrome grooved trim and bumpers, cable-operated hood release and round horn grilles.

Above right: In contrast to the Hebmüller version, the Karmann cabriolet was a four-seater, introduced with the Export sedan in 1949.

Right: Once the horn was mounted behind the fender, these grilles became necessary. They were circular until October 1952.

Bumpers were now chromed with a groove along the center and the new style hubcaps with their bigger VW badge were chromed too. The new bright trim (chrome plated brass) extended along the sides of the body and down the center of the hood, which also gained a bright VW badge at the top end of the chrome trim. To silence complaints about engine noise, Export models had better sound-deadening in the engine compartment, while at the other end, they moved the horn from behind the front bumper to beneath the front left-hand wing to give the front a less cluttered look. To make sure the horn blast could be heard properly, a small round grille was introduced to the bottom of both fenders; the dummy (without a hole behind it) right hand one was obviously just to balance the one on the left. For improved interior comfort, the Export models had better trim with adjustable front seats and arm rests for both front and rear passengers. There were even optional bolster cushions, shaped like giant sausages with pretty gathered ends. The Export instrument panel was an ivory color with matching knobs and a new white two-spoked steering wheel, and there was even an optional clock to fill the right-hand dash space. The starter button was in the middle of the dash just below the pull-out ashtray and, interestingly, the interior light was switched on from the windscreen wiper control.

Until the late 1960s, the Volkswagen's biggest export markets were the USA and Holland, and it was a Dutch car dealer, Mr Ben Pon who introduced the first official Beetle imports into both countries. Pon had been keen to own a Volkswagen dealership since before the war, but he didn't get his hands on one until 1946, when he managed to get ten secondhand cars back to Holland. Although everyone was clamoring for new cars in the immediate post-war period, there was still a lot of anti-German feeling throughout the world, which obviously didn't do great things for sales. But in the light of severely restricted production, actually getting them in the first place was more of a problem than selling them once he'd taken delivery. By 1948, new Beetles were leaving Pon's dealership virtually the minute they arrived, so it was only natural that he should begin looking for new markets. Leaving Holland on the M/S Westerdam, he docked in New York on 17 January 1949 with the first officially imported Beetle.

With the United States graduating towards ever bigger and more powerful cars, and the fact that the press only ever referred to it as 'Hitler's car', it was no surprise that Pon came away with no dealers whatsoever. He even had to sell the car for $800 to pay his hotel bill. Later that year, Nordhoff himself flew to New York with assorted photographs of the car to try the same approach, but again nothing happened. In fact, the customs inspector at the airport refused to believe that they were photographs of a real car and made him pay duty on them as advertising artwork. It was not until 1950 that the first exclusive Volkswagen importer and agent for the United States East of the Mississippi was appointed. His name was Max Hoffman.

Hoffman added the Volkswagen to the other (Porsche and Jaguar) import dealerships at his Park Avenue premises. He offered four versions, the Standard, De Luxe (Export model), De Luxe with sunroof and the Convertible. Price ran from $1280 to $1997 for the rag top. From selling only two Volkswagens in America in 1949, they managed 330 in 1950, growing to 980 by 1953, when Volkswagen canceled Hoffman's franchise. By then, a Mr John von Neumann had been appointed agent for the Western States and was proving far more enthusiastic about the product. Hoffman was more interested in wholesaling and Nordhoff wanted more control over setting up a proper nationwide sales and service network.

If the 1940s was the decade of recovery, the 1950s was the decade that saw the Beetle consolidated as a major player throughout the world automotive market. Production soared and the car became better and more re-

Above: New for 1950 was the Type 2 Volkswagen Transporter. This is a beautifully restored ambulance version.

Left: You can't help but wonder what the roof rack was for, along with its side-mount ladder. Maybe a couple of extra patients?

Above right: Another expertly restored Type 2, this time the pickup version with its drop-down sides.

Far right: Finally, the Transporter van version, with opening side doors and rare opening 'safari' windshields.

Right: A 1950 Export model with the new sunroof. The optional opening rear windows really were as bad as they looked and only lasted a year.

fined. Daily output was around 312 in 1950, by 1955 it was almost 1000 and by 1960, total German Beetle output would hit 725,927.

1950 was not only a milestone year for the Beetle (4 March saw the 100,000th), but a new Volkswagen plant was opened at Brunswick and even a new model, the Type 2 Transporter was produced. This boxy, commercial design based on the familiar Beetle mechanics, began as a simple van but soon stretched the range to take in many other bodystyles from pickups to people carriers, campers and ambulances.

In every way the Beetle was becoming more refined. In April 1950 there came an optional full-length canvas sunroof, which provided the fresh air of a convertible when needed or the closed comfort of the sedan. Sunroofs were manufactured by the German Golde company but installed by Volkswagen on the production line. They took the form of a canvas top with ribs that slid in tracks at the two sides to sit neatly on the back of the roof, and there were various designs over the years. The earliest version came in cloth with four square corners, then after 1955 it was shortened slightly with rounded front corners. In August 1956 it was lengthened again and in September 1956 it was changed to vinyl before the introduction of the new sliding steel sunroof in 1964. Another option in 1950 were rear vent windows, but they were ob-

viously not too much of a success as they were replaced on 1 June 1951 by small vents in the front quarter panels. Instead of the rear passengers' ears getting the draught, the front passengers' legs did. This was hardly the best of ideas either, and once again it lasted just one year, to be replaced in October 1952 by the far more sensible front window vents.

By now the engine was fitted with a simple mechanical thermostat in the form of a sort of bellows that would heat up and open various flaps to allow more cooling air around the cylinder barrels. Volkswagen also introduced the 'Autothermik' pistons with offset piston pins to held reduce piston slap. Along with better valve seals and exhaust valves, they helped improve the engine's overall reputation.

Incredibly, it was not until 1950 that the first major modifications and improvements in the braking system took place. In April the Export model was lucky enough to get proper hydraulic brakes with its combined master cylinder/reservoir just below the fuel tank. The 1200 Standard however, kept mechanical brakes until 1964. In reality, there were few brake modifications over the years, more in the way of detail changes than anything else. Front linings were made wider (30mm to 40mm) in 1957, front and rear brake cylinder bores were increased at the same time and then decreased in 1967

Left: Restored 1950 Export model shows split rear window and the attractive curves that were lost as the car got older.

Far left: The spare wheel tool kit was a popular and very handy accessory. From 1950 the horn grilles were plated.

Below: From inside the split rear window never exactly gave the best rear vision. The interior light was originally operated from the windshield wiper switch!

Above right: The Export dashboard brought in new ivory-colored dashboard panels and two-spoke steering wheel.

Right: Although this is the 1951 engine with fixed generator pedestal, it also benefits from some additional parts from Okrasa, one of the earliest suppliers of Volkswagen tuning gear.

back to 17.5mm. Disk brakes were not used until 1967 and even then it was only on certain models.

Setting the style for every future Beetle, the aluminum crankcase was replaced with the new magnesium alloy (Elektron) one in 1951 and in March of that year they also swapped to single valve springs to reduce the reciprocating weight and, no doubt, the number of parts that might break. The new Solex 28PCI carburetor with its built-in accelerator pump mechanism and new inlet manifold, helped eradicate the reported acceleration flat spots, too.

Updates elsewhere were few and far between in 1951. Notable additions were that export Beetles gained a few fine details on their trim: a chrome strip was added to the windshield surround in April, while the nose of the hood gained the attractive little Wolfsburg crest with its castle, wolf and water, slotted on to the bottom end of the chrome trim, just above the polished aluminum hood handle.

In contrast, 1952 was a much busier year in the new features department. Production of new cars had now passed 100,000 per year and each new feature brought new customers in more countries around the globe. The major change was in the interior. The dashboard was redesigned (some would say for the worse) and lost most of the character of the old one, not to mention the amount of storage space. The speedometer (there was no fuel guage until 1962), was now mounted straight into a flat dash panel, with a centrally-mounted rectangular grill which had provision for a radio speaker to be mounted behind it. There was also room for an optional radio mounted in the underdash area, filled with a blanking plate, and even a special lump in the car's roof panel just above the windshield, which took the top radio aerial mount. The aerial was a strange contraption extending down past the center of the windshield with a bottom mount on the cowl. It is worth noting at this point that the new dashboard is usually associated with the 1953 change from a split rear window to the oval shape. But because the dash alteration

Above left: The Wolfsburg badge was first seen on the 1951 Export model and decorated Beetle hoods until 1962.

Above: The temperamental semaphore turn signals lasted until 1961, when they were replaced by fender mounted indicators.

Left: Part of the 1952 interior update was this new dashboard with central radio grille, ashtray and separate starter button to the left of the speedo.

Above right: The 1951 Export Beetle is notable for its front quarter panel air vents.

Right: Can there be many better views for a Beetle enthusiast?

came in October 1952 and the oval window wasn't introduced until March of the following year, there are some split-window Beetles with the later style dash.

Another new feature was the glove compartment lid, opened by a tiny button. Glove box lids had been standard on Beetle Cabriolets before, but only optional on sedans. There was a small ashtray on the new dash, flush-mounted and painted to match. And the control for the semaphores was moved on to the steering column like a normal indicator stalk, but fixed to the side of the column with a metal strap.

Until now, operating the windows had been a major chore, but a new mechanism was fitted so that it now only required 3.5 turns to fully lift the window, not a ridiculous 10.5 as before. The interior light was moved from the back to the nearside, just above the door pillar and the rear view mirror became more rounded in shape.

On the outside 1952 saw new windshield wipers. Previously they possessed the crudest thin wire arms, driven by a small electric motor under the cowl. The new arms had a flat profile and they even self-parked. The proper vent windows introduced in 1952, not only replaced the front leg-level vents, but they also superceded another method of controled ventilation – the small cutouts in the front top corner of the windows that would let in a little air if you opened them just slightly. From October, the front horn grilles were an oval shape, and chrome-plated on the Export cars, a feature which lasted on 1200cc models right up to July 1973, though they were later swapped for a lightweight aluminum alloy pressing.

At the back, the engine cover now got a T-handle, replacing the previous loop type and the old 'pope's nose' rear light was swapped for a new one – still quite nosey, but fatter and less Roman-looking. The new light dispensed with the stop light too, as this facility was transferred to the two rear fender taillights. Replacing the rather pointy-looking single red marker lights, these attractive little units had a small red oval main light face with the stop light as a yellow heart-shaped window in the top. Export rear lights had been slightly different (with a chrome ring) from around 1949. Indicators were still the semaphores in the door pillar.

On the mechanical side, October 1952 also saw the old 16 inch wheels being replaced by a wider (at 4 inches) 15 inch rim, which gave rise to changes in the transmission ratios, though they were already slightly different between Standard and Export models anyway. The new transmission on the Export model also received synchromesh on second, third and fourth

gears. To help ride and handling, six-leaf front torsion bars were introduced (later changed again to 8 leaves in 1953), the suspension travel was extended by some 30mm to 135mm and the size of the rear torsion bars were reduced at the same time.

Although 1953 is regarded by many as a great cutoff year, marking the end of the famous 'pretzel' split rear window (the last split-window Beetle was built on 10 March), it was hardly a remarkable year in terms of body work changes overall. A lock-button was added to the vent window catches and the brake master cylinder reservoir was relocated. The new steel reservoir pot now sat on the shelf behind the spare tire under the hood. By now the real chromed steel trim was swapped for polished aluminum alloy.

Far more significant that year was the growth in foreign markets. The first of the big subsidiaries, Volkswagen do Brazil was set up in Ipiranga, Sao Paulo in March 1953, and the first Beetle was imported into Nigeria through Mandilas Ltd, a former Jaguar agent, who distributed their cars until 1974 when Volkswagen of Nigeria came into being.

Australia was another country to fall to the all-conquering Volkswagen, though it never really caught on as it did in other areas. The first-ever Australian Volkswagen was imported in 1951, a 1946 model taken over as part of the possessions of one Therese Hanael. Official imports began in 1953, and in 1954, Martin and King Pty Ltd began assembling CKD (Completely Knocked Down) Beetles in Melbourne. It didn't take long for the by-now Volkswagen (Australasia) Pty Ltd to capture 10 percent of the sedan car market, passing that goal in 1954. In 1960, when they produced their own 1200 Beetle model, 80 percent of it originated in Australia. The 100,000th Australian Beetle left the line in 1961 and was swapped with the Hanael's original 1946 for the VW museum. Yet despite achieving their 200,000th car in 1964 with grand plans for bigger and better manufacturing plants, the Melbourne facility returned to CKD assembly in 1967 and the plant was finally sold to Datsun in 1975. All was not lost, however, as the tooling was sold to Indonesia and production continued there.

There had been a small but steady trickle of Volkswagens into Great Britain after the war, but on 1 January 1953, the official import franchise was awarded to an Irishman, Stephen O'Flaherty, in the name of Volkswagen Motors Ltd. Once Nordhoff had decided that the British agency should be British-owned to combat the strong anti-German feeling, it was no surprise that they chose O'Flaherty, who had been building CKD Beetles at his Dublin-based factory since 1951. It was actually the first foreign plant to do so. There had been a British importer before 1953, but Volkswagen had only given him a very limited franchise.

A J Colborne-Baber had been selling 'reconditioned' Beetles from his garage in Ripley, Surrey since 1948, mainly second-hand Forces' cars that had been resprayed and retrimmed in leather. In 1951, one such sedan would have cost £410, or £425 if converted to right-hand drive. In early 1952 this was formalised into a franchise to sell new Volkswagens and VW spare parts, but only to overseas visitors, usually US Air Force personnel stationed in Kent.

O'Flaherty's new unlimited franchise meant an initial order for 200 cars and new applications for dealerships (many were ex-dealers of the recently folded Jowett company of Bradford, Yorkshire). New cars arrived in batches of 20 along with £10 worth of spares each.

From humble premises in Bedford Street, London, to offices above the Lotus showroom in Regent Street, they moved on to a showroom in St James's Street, with the offices and spares storage in the basement below. Eventually 50,000 square feet of disused railway sheds in Plaistow became

Above left: After October 1952 the Export model gained front vent windows, and 15-inch wheels. The chrome trim was no longer fluted.

Left: At the rear the cars lost the 'Popes Nose' light, and the rear stop lights gained the heart-shaped lenses in the top after October 1952.

Above: This right-hand drive Export car shows how the dashboard was simply reversed. Note the space for the optional radio with its blanking plate.

Right: In 1953 Beetles still had to make do with the last of the 25 horsepower 1131cc motor, until January 1954 brought the 1192cc 30 horse unit.

Above: New in March 1953 was the oval rear window. This is an American spec car with the pram-handle bumpers.

Left: This 1954 sedan not only carries 1962-67 rear lights, but a VW Type 4 engine with modified flat fan and pulley arrangement.

Right: Once retracted, the Golde sunroof gave passengers almost as much air as the cabriolet. For 1956 the sunroof became plastic instead of cloth.

home for the spare parts warehouse. Sales went from just 945 Volkswagens in 1953 to 3260 the next year and around 5000 a year until the end of the 1950s when sales reached almost 10,000 vehicles a year. By then there was no doubt. The Volkswagen had well and truly arrived in Britain.

The first increase in engine power for over ten years came in 1954 as capacity was raised from 1131cc to 1192cc, achieved by increasing the bore slightly from 75 to 77mm. At the same time, the engine got larger inlet valves (28 to 30mm), compression was raised to 6:1 and the cylinder heads were redesigned for better flow with more fins for better cooling. The distributor now came with additional vacuum advance too, all of which came together to squeeze out another 5hp – 30hp at 3400rpm. The last 25 horsepower engine appeared literally on the last day of 1953. *Autocar* Magazine's 1954 Beetle test noted a maximum speed of 62.5mph with 0-50mph (60mph was presumably too long a wait) of 22.2 seconds, a slight improvement on the old 1953 figure of 22.9, but still nothing to become excited about. Overall fuel consumption was logged at 34.5mph, worse than the previous 37.7, but the kerbweight was up that year by some 60lb.

Inside the car the starter, which had previously been a separate button to the left of the speedo, was now incorporated into the ignition switch, the ashtray gained a smart chrome trim and there were buttons in the door jambs for the automatic courtesy light. The seats were made slightly more comfortable and the rear one was slimmed to give passengers more room.

On the outside, the new style rear lamps ditched the heart-shaped lens in response to American laws. The lamp itself became larger to house a double filament bulb. In August of the following year, Volkswagen moved the rear lamps two inches up the fenders to make them more visible. 1954 was also the last year the Americans had semaphore turn signals, replaced in 1955 by small bullet-shaped indicators mounted low down on the front fenders to the outside of the headlamps.

With 1955 heralding the change in model year designation, the 1956 model year began immediately after the factory's summer shutdown in August 1955. And although sales were continuing their phenomenal rise (the

millionth Beetle was built in August 1955), there was little to shout about at Wolfsburg in terms of model changes throughout the late fifties. Apart from the changes we've already mentioned in taillight location and sunroof fabric, little happened until 1958 really, when the small oval rear window finally disappeared.

The last Beetle with a single exhaust pipe, appeared on 31 July 1955, replaced by twin tailpipes, chromed on Export cars, black enamel on the Standard model. Other engine modifications included a larger oil pump drive to reduce engine wear and later, in January 1957, the size of the internal oil passages were increased for the same reason. October 1957 saw new damp-resistant sound proofing in the engine compartment, while at the front, a new fuel tank gave Beetle drivers slightly more luggage space, yet retained almost the same fuel capacity.

In America the 'plumbers' delight' protective bumpers were introduced in 1956, which built on the basic European blade bumpers by the addition of round tube 'handles', passing through the overriders, curving down to plug back into the bumper and braced to the body with yet further tubes. The front had one tube, running right across the length of the bumper blade, the rear came with two tubes, one on each side. The gap was to allow opening of the engine lid.

In terms of interior upgrading, 1956 saw a cranked shift lever to allow the heater control to be moved forward, and the front seats were widened by 1¼ inches. They even had three-position adjustment for the backs, by means of an eccentric knob. To allow the driver to get a decent view of his speedometer, the steering wheel spokes were lowered so they sprouted out of the bottom of the central boss, and to aid with proper door location, new adjustable striker plates were introduced in 1957. At the same time, the two front outlets were moved back, nearer to the door posts with slotted louvers replacing the old chicken wire covers.

Increasing the Volkswagen range as a method of selling more vehicles, in 1956 the Osnabrück-based Karmann company, who were already producing the Volkswagen Convertibles, released a totally new sporty model based on

Previous pages: The millionth Beetle is cheered off the line on 5 August 1955.

Above: From the 1956 brochure, a picture of the Karmann Cabriolet that you certainly wouldn't get away with nowadays.

Left: In 1956 the new steering wheel had off-center spokes to allow a better view of the speedometer. There was also a cranked shifter and a handle for the ashtray.

Right: The license plate says it all. Note the US bumpers and the accessory roofrack. By 1958 that oval rear window would be history.

Beetle mechanics. Designed by the Italian styling house, Ghia, and mounted on what was a slightly wider Beetle export chassis, it featured attractive, swoopy lines, and was mostly hand-finished, giving it the flavor and finish of many of its Italian peers, but the simplicity and reliability of its Volkswagen heritage. There were four Karmann-Ghia models, the 143 and 144 being the left- and right-hand drive coupés, the 141 and 142 being two convertible versions. In its first four years, sales rose from 500 to 6000 a year. And as production rose, Nordhoff actually passed the economies on to the customers, reducing the prices in 1961.

New factories appeared and others were improved at this time too. The Hanover factory produced its first Type 2 in March 1956 (later it would become a major engine plant), while another plant at Kassel became operational on 1 July for making drive-line parts and reconditioning factory engines and transmissions. Extending to over 400 acres, Nordhoff had the Kassel factory repaired from its wartime bombing damage and at the same time expanded and modernized it.

In 1958 the Beetle lost the famous small oval rear window, increasing rear visibility by a sizeable amount and at the same time reducing the rear air intakes in size. With the new 'modern' rear window came other styling modifications. The windshield was enlarged to match the rear window, and the beautiful curvy lines of the old engine cover were changed for a simpler (less distinctive) design which a flat license plate fitted more neatly. To accommodate its altered contours, there was yet another license plate light too. As was the company practice, the last oval windowed Beetle was built on 31 July (chassis license 1-600 439), just before the summer shutdown and model change.

Although the decade was nowhere near over, the Beetle had finally shaken off much of its early, outdated, vintage looks and was set for even greater things in the 1960s. Production had risen to over 380,000 by the end of 1958, and by the end of 1968, annual production would be way over the million units per year. The Wolfsburg workers had learned their lessons in hard work, but they still had a long way to go yet. Nordhoff would see to that.

Left: New for 1958, the full-width rear window brought with it new rear lights, and a new engine lid.

Below left: 1958 Sunroof model. Few bodywork change took place between 1958 and the demise of the semaphore turn signals in 1961.

Right: Little happened in the engine department in the late 1950s either. This is a 1958 model with the 1192cc unit and twin exhaust pipes.

Below right: German 1958 sedan. A few accessories brighten up the basic Beetle.

New Models & Markets

Restyled and ready for the sixties, the 1958 Beetle may have had a more modern look, but there were many who thought the Beetle body design was past its best. Others thought it was time for a totally new model altogether, but Nordhoff was not one of them. After all, every year he increased the Beetle production targets and every year they beat them. Why should they upset the apple cart with anything radical? Launching a replacement was extremely risky and even with Volkswagen's reputation, success was not always guaranteed (as they would find with most of their new models). The total production tally for 1958 was 451,526 and by 1959 the total output of German Beetles had reached 575,407 with another 8383 built at the fast growing Brazilian plant.

To emphasize the fact that here was a new-style Beetle, the 1958 model carried another new dashboard. The radio grille was restyled with vertical not horizontal slats, and moved so that it now enveloped the whole of the speedo, right in front of the driver. The glovebox was much larger and there was now a radio slot in the center of the dash instead of below it. A wide chrome strip went right across the center of the fascia, adding to the bright chrome of the speedometer bezel. The steering wheel was still the same old two-spoker, but it wouldn't last long and there was even a 'normal' accelerator pedal for 1958, replacing the old-fashioned, unsuccessful roller pedal.

Despite the fact that Volkswagen couldn't build the cars fast enough, in 1959 Dr Carl Hahn (head of US operations) decided that the time had come for a little product promotion. The word was put out to all the big Madison Avenue agencies to pitch for the initial $800,000 account. And after listening to endless companies not only saying the same as each other, but the same as they did for every other car on the market, Hahn went for the relatively small agency, Doyle Dane Bernbach.

The campaign was different in so many ways. For a start, the presentation of each advertisement followed a simple formula that has since been recognized as the basis for 'good' advertising by agencies the world over. A simple picture of the car (though once or twice just a blank space), a simple easy-to-understand line beneath it and three columns of simple, informative copy. Where it differed was in its 'soft sell.' They didn't try to push the car at you, tell you how beautiful it was, that it would never break down, or that it was the newest, best styled car on the road. They just told the truth. And to ensure this, they sent an army of copywriters, artists, account executives

and assorted other agency people over to Wolfsburg to actually see for themselves how Volkswagen built Volkswagens. Not only did this give them the intimate knowledge of the car's design and construction that formed the basis of so many of the ads, but it taught them about the care and attention that went into each and every car; one of Nordhoff's original company aims and one that, again, figures strongly in the advertising.

'Lemon' claimed one ad, beneath a picture of what looked for all the world like a perfectly ordinary Beetle. You read, however, that a small blemish on the glove compartment chrome strip had caused it to fail inspection.

'After a few years, it starts to look beautiful,' claimed another, beneath a picture of the car nose on, photographed with a wide-angle lens to make it look even odder. Fortunately the copy reminded us that a Volkswagen retained its value better than any other car on the road, which along with other benefits, were quite enough to make it beautiful. There again, how many other car companies begin an advertisement by describing their own car with the words, 'ugly', 'no class', 'afterthought' and 'El-Pig-O'?

Needless to say, the TV commercials that followed were just as interesting to watch, just as informative and just as successful. By then the account was worth $20 million a year, but by then they needed it too. With sales of imported cars peaking in 1959, the Americans were starting to react. The groundswell of anti-foreign car feeling was growing, mainly from a desire to protect the ailing American car and steel industries. And the American 'compact' was on the way.

Sales of European cars to the USA were almost halved in 1961, yet Volkswagen captured 46 percent of the total import market. This must say something for both the car and its advertising. In 1960, America imported its 500,000th vehicle.

At home, ever more investment led to even greater production levels. Another 500 million Deutschmarks in 1960 helped production increase by as much as 100 vehicles a day. By now the company employed some 54,000 people and more than a third of all cars in Germany were Volkswagens. Demand was still high and output was growing to match it. So to give the German people a share in the company's phenomenal success, changes were made in its corporate structure allowing 60 percent of its shares to be offered for sale on the German stock exchange. Volkswagen GmbH had now become Volkswagen AG.

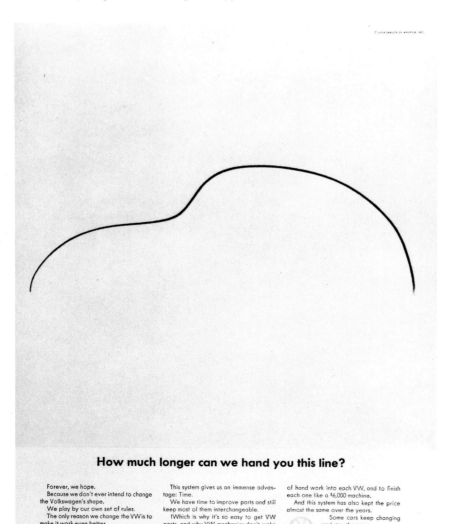

How much longer can we hand you this line?

Need a part?

© VOLKSWAGEN OF AMERICA, INC.

How to make a '54 look like a '64.

Paint it.

See? It looks like next year's model.

And next year's model looks like last year's model. And so it goes.

VWs always look the same because we change the car only to make it work better, never to make it look different.

So the people who bought '63 VWs aren't nervous about what the '64s will look like. And neither are we.

We've made over 5 million Volkswagens, and we're still making changes.

Not enough to make you run out and buy a new one every year.

But enough to notice the differences when you do. (14 changes for '64 alone.)

In the meantime, no matter what year VW you own, you can always get parts easily; many of them are interchangeable from one year to the next.

 So if you like, you can keep your old VW running forever. Just spray it every few years. Old paint rides again.

CONVERTIBLE

Left: From the 1959 catalog, more artistic impressions of the Beetle Convertible with totally the wrong curves.

Right: Wolfsburg. The factory is on one side of the tracks, the town on the other.

Below and previous pages: Classic Volkswagen advertising from Doyle Dane Bernbach, setting a whole new style in automotive advertising.

There were still few product improvements of a major nature at this time, and what few there were just followed the same old tack of gradual evolution of the basic commodity. Following the American lead, European Beetles lost their semaphores in 1960, though were replaced by slim chromed indicators mounted on top of the front fenders. At the rear, indicators were incorporated into the small lights. Another 'modernization' was the introduction of new exterior door handles with square pushbuttons. Eagle-eyed Volkswagen enthusiasts will note that for 1960 only, the key slot was vertical, after which it became horizontal. And the passenger side, as ever, had no exterior

locking facility, and the Wolfsburg crest was also imperceptibly altered.

For the first time in many years, the 1960 Beetle also got the benefit of improved ride and handling. The transmission swing-axle pivot was lowered by tipping the engine and transmission forward two degrees (which also required a modified exhaust system), a hydraulic steering damper was fitted for the first time and the front torsion bar end bushes were changed to needle rollers. There was even a front stabilizer for the Export models along with thinner and shorter rear torsion bars, all of which came together to improve handling by an appreciable amount.

It makes your house look bigger.

You're missing a lot when you own a Volkswagen.

Inside the car the updated steering wheel eventually made an appearance: a larger dished design with a finely sculpted chrome half horn ring. At the same time, the front seat backs were contoured for even further passenger comfort and there was a new padded leathercloth sun visor instead of the old green plastic one. Front passengers now had a foot rest, too.

By 5 December 1961, Volkswagen production had reached 5 million, just 14 years after Nordhoff had taken up the company reins. The milestone Beetle was presented to the International Red Cross and to mark the occasion, the Bavarian mint issued gold and silver coins with a profile of the car on one side and of Nordhoff on the other. His speech reiterated that continuing technical excellence, quality and value were at the root of the company's success and would continue as primary aims. In his work, Nordhoff himself showed the example as a tireless pusher, questioner and thinker, totally impatient with incompetence.

By now the plant he had reconstructed from ruins had become massive, with figures bordering on the unbelievable: 10.8 million square feet of factory, around 270 acres of roofed production area, 110 miles of continuous flow conveyor lines, 31.2 miles of railway track and daily production of well over 5000 vehicles. Certainly a far cry from the day Nordhoff had taken over when the factory had no roof and production was barely 5000 a year.

For 1961, the Beetle engine had been totally redesigned. The new 34hp engine achieved a 13 percent increase in power through a number of detail modifications, most of which had been introduced on the Type 2 Transporter the year earlier. Using the same bore and stroke, VW engineers raised the compression again to 7:1 and fitted a new Solex 28 PICT carburetor with automatic choke and a system of pipes to the left-hand heater junction box to help prevent icing in the winter. The dynamo support stand was now a separate item and the fuel pump was moved to the top of the crankcase. The

spark plugs no longer ran in a steel tube and the new distributor dispensed with its mechanical advance weights, relying solely on a vacuum for the advance mechanism. The crankcase itself was redesigned, obviously because the previous dynamo pedestal had been integral with the right-hand half, so they made it stronger all round and enlarged the bearing area.

To ensure it was up to the job, the drive line was also redesigned with synchromesh for first gear and new ratios all round. Acceleration was obviously improved as a result of this, in fact it was fast enough for *Autocar* to record a 0-60mph time in 1960: 32.1 seconds, with only 17.7 seconds to 50mph, a marked improvement on the previous effort. Top speed was up at 72mph but again, average fuel consumption was down at only 31.6mpg. Although it had no extra capacity, they redesigned the fuel tank that year, which increased luggage space under the sloping hood by an incredible 65 percent.

Other new features included a windshield washer system, with a white plastic washer bottle concealed behind the spare tire, next to the new style 'quick check' brake fluid reservoir. The system was pressurized by hand from a hand-pump on the dash. A grab handle and sunvisor for front seat passengers and longer front seat runners to allow more leg room were also introduced.

In 1961 Volkswagen launched a new model, an attempt to take the basic Beetle design upmarket and maybe even to test the water for a replacement. Though it kept to Volkswagen principles with a separate floorpan, torsion bar suspension and a rear-mounted air-cooled engine, the Type 3 (though it was launched simply as the Volkswagen 1500) was much more in keeping with contemporary styling. It looked better, rode and handled better, and certainly offered much improved interior comfort. You did have to pay for the privilege, however. In May 1963, when the 'Volkswagen VW 1500 Estate car' (station wagon) was still relatively new to Britain, it would have set you back

Above left: A 1961 in beautiful condition, right down to the period accessories.

Above: 1961 brought a new engine in the form of the 34hp unit with its raised compression and new Solex 28 PICT carburetor.

Right: The interior was updated in the early 1960s to take in contoured seats and the new style dished steering wheel with its chromed half horn-ring. 1961 saw the first passenger interior grab handles.

£997. The new Ford Consul Cortina ('Beautifully made – to go fast!') cost around £600.

Many versions of the Type 3 were available, from a two-door sedan, a station wagon and a rather sharp-edged two-door Karmann-Ghia version, to a still-born convertible based on the sedan. It is interesting that this very attractive and stylish convertible even appeared in the launch brochure, but was canceled at the last minute, presumably due to lack of rigidity in the bodyshell. It wasn't long before a fastback version was also added to the range. The engine was a 1493cc four-cylinder unit, using Beetle-type components, but with a flat fan instead of the upright Beetle type. This gave the Type 3 the rare honor of luggage space at the back as well as in the front underhood area. The rear 'trunk' was opened with a cable-pull lever, secreted in the driver's (LHD) door jamb and featured a removable hatch for rather cramped access to the engine. Despite the fact that in many respects it was a far better car, certainly in terms of ride and comfort, space and luggage capacity, the Type 3 never really gained the following the Beetle had, though it did last in a restyled form (after 1966) until 1973 after some 2.3 million units.

By 1961 56 percent of total Volkswagen output was exported and annual German production exceeded a million vehicles, over three-quarters of them Beetles. In Britain, sales had grown to such a point that the German-built cars were supplemented by additional right-hand drive cars built in Brussels, Belgium from CKD kits. The range at this time included the 1200 Standard and Export sedan plus the cabriolet.

One of the many design features that had managed to last from year to

year despite complaints from the driving public, was the hood stay, a simple over-center lever on the right of the hood. To close them, absent minded owners would yank on their hoods, forgetting that the lever had to be released first, resulting more often than not in a creased hood. In 1962 the introduction of the new spring-loaded hinges for both sides cured the problem at a stroke.

Another major area of driver dissent was the lack of a fuel gauge. By 1962 this had probably become so much of an embarrassment for Volkswagen, that they had to remedy the situation. It may have looked like an afterthought, tacked on to the dashboard just to the right of the speedo, but that's exactly what it was. And I'm sure nobody complained. A small styling flaw was a small price to pay for the luxury of knowing how much fuel you had left. Obviously, the reservoir fuel tap with its bulkhead remote control lever became obsolete and was withdrawn.

The recently introduced washer system was modified in 1962 to take pressure from the spare tyre. A sticker warned drivers not to inflate the plastic bottle beyond 35 lb/square inch for obvious reasons.

Mechanically, the 1962 Beetle adopted 'maintenance-free' clutch and handbrake cables and a new worm and roller steering box to replace the old worm and nut box, which apart from a couple of minor changes had stayed virtually the same since 1945. The new box was accompanied by new 'maintenance-free' adjustable track rods.

On the outside, a new rear light cluster incorporated tail, stop and indicators in the one large light unit, and new door restraining straps were introduced. The interior gained sliding covers for the front heating outlets, an outlet for the rear passengers and even seat belt mountings, though they didn't go as far as to provide the belts themselves which remained an accessory for many years yet to come.

Accessories had been an important part of Beetle motoring for almost as long as there had been Beetles. Like some were supplied by the factory and were available through local dealerships, while many more were manufactured by independent companies who realized that there was always someone who wanted their car slightly improved or personalized to a better standard than the factory could offer.

For a car as basic as the Beetle, there were probably more accessories than most. In the very early days, clocks were the big seller, with different types to fit the varying styles of dashboard through the years. The central radio grille of the 1953 style dashboard was often replaced by a new version with integral clock, or even swapped totally for a sporty set of three instruments including fuel and oil pressure gauges.

Radios were, of course, another popular dealer-fitted accessory, beginning with the beautiful Telefunken sets from 1949 to 1952, and moving up through a variety of styles and manufacturers: Blaupunkt, Akkord and Bendix (later they were rebadged as Volkswagen radios) with aerials to match,

Previous pages: 1964 Cabriolet in Ruby Red. Note how the engine cover incorporates the engine cooling louvers.

Left: US-spec sloping headlamps differed from the European ones in that the sloping cover glass was clear with a separate light lens set behind.

Above: Volkswagen Type 3 in Fastback form. The Fastback didn't actually appear until after the sedan (Notchback) and station wagon (Squareback) versions were in production.

Right: The still-born VW 1500 Cabriolet. Although this car appeared in the first Type 3 brochure, the car was never produced for the public.

usually from Bosch. There were both fuel cans and tool kits, specially shaped to fit inside the spare wheel, while driving lamps, dashboard flower vases, mud guards, additional sun visors, under-dash package trays, an endless variety of chrome dress-up parts and rear view mirrors, even air conditioning and a 45rpm slot-in record player were all available to Beetle drivers at some point in the car's life.

Perhaps because they were saving it all up for later, little happened to the Beetle in terms of improvements for 1963 or 1964. 1963 sadly spelt the end of the hood-mounted Wolfsburg crest, a perforated vinyl roof liner was brought in to match the recently introduced trim cloth, and adhesive anti-drumming foam was added to the floors for added sound insulation.

In 1964, the old PVC sunroof was replaced with a crank-driven steel one, the horn ring disappeared for a simple thumb-operated bar, set into the steering wheel spokes and the engine cover received a new, wider license plate light.

Minor engineering modifications included larger diameter link pins and the Type 3 1500 stub axles. The Type 3 was to provide further suspension improvements later in 1966 when the link pins were dropped altogether in favor of ball-joints. Incredibly, this single update increased service periods from 1500 to 6000 miles, and then all they needed was the odd squirt of grease. Sadly, the two front ends weren't interchangeable as the new version's torsion tubes were further apart.

At this time, Beetles could be ordered in some of the most beautiful colors. The four new ones for 1964 came with exciting, evocative names: Panama Beige, Java Green, Bahama Blue and Sea Blue; Pearl White, Anthracite, Black and Ruby Red were continued from 1963.

Beetle production had reached over 800,000 a year by now and the million cars a year barrier was just around the corner. Nordhoff opened yet another factory in 1964 at Emden, a North Sea port, chosen because it was handy for exports mainly to the USA where sales were still massive. By the time the factory became operational on 1 December, US sales had reached over 276,000 and continued to rise until 1968 when increased competition from more modern US and Japanese 'compact' cars took its toll.

There were plans for more foreign production facilities this year, too. Volkswagen de Mexico was established in January and production of the 1200 began very quickly. That same car continued with very few changes right into the 1980s and it would be this plant at Pueblo, that would supply the European market once the German facility had ceased production, though the Mexican Beetle was obviously far less refined.

Not every government was happy for Volkswagen to send kits of Beetle parts to be assembled in foreign plants, though. To encourage industrial development across a whole spectrum of activities, the South African government brought in a new regulation that 55 percent of each car manufactured

Left: A car for all seasons. Note the US-spec headlamps, bumpers and no front license plate.

Above: US-spec bumpers featured extra bumper irons which bolted through the fenders. Pearl white was not a stock color.

Above right: Spot the accessory.

Right: 1967 was the year Volkswagen lost its European number one sales position to Fiat.

Left: 1965 was the year that saw increased window area and thinner screen pillars.

Right: 1967 was more remarkable for the changes it brought in the engineering department, than anything on the outside of the car, though this humble 1200 saw little or no change.

Below right: By 1967 the engine cover had been restyled for a smoother look.

Below far right: 1967 also marked the last year of the push-button door handles, as they were changed for a trigger mechanism in 1968.

had to be of South African origin. Volkswagen's reply was to take total control of the South African production facility at Uitenhage. A company by the name of SAMAD (South African Motor Assemblers and Distributors Ltd) had put together CKD Beetles since August 1951 alongside American Studebakers and even the odd Austin, but only Volkswagen had the wherewithall to comply with the new regulations and the new company became known as Volkswagen of South Africa. Over the years, South African output began with the 1200, increasing engine capacity to 1285cc in 1966 and then to 1493cc only a year later. There were also assorted specials produced after 1974, including the Jeans Beetle (with denim trim). South African production peaked at around 21,000 in 1973 and ended in January 1979 to make way for the Golf.

Growth came from other directions too. As if opening new production facilities around the world wasn't enough, further major expansion began on 5 January 1964, when Volkswagenwerk AG bought Auto Union of Ingolstadt from Daimler-Benz who had owned it since 1958. The Auto Union was just that, formed by the union of Audi, DKW, Horch and Wanderer. Volkswagen only used the name Audi, of course, for the new range that would take some of the financial pressure off Nordhoff to replace the Beetle. In addition they had bought in all that valuable experience in 'conventional' cars like the Audi 70, that the company would need to survive through the 1970s.

Yet further Beetle assembly at the newly acquired Ingolstadt factory helped to take Beetle production to 1,008,983 in 1965, with the ten millionth Volkswagen leaving the line at Wolfsburg only four years after the five millionth.

1965 also saw changes in the Beetle bodyshell the likes of which had not been seen since the loss of the oval rear window in 1958. The difference was again in increased window area. The windshield grew by 11 percent and at the same time was given a slight curve and longer windshield wipers which parked at the left. The door glass was six percent bigger and the rear side glass 17.5 percent larger thanks to slimmer pillars and an extra inch in depth. The rear screen gained a further 19.5 percent more glass area. A new push-button lock replaced the old engine cover T-handle, while the old pushbutton vent windows locks were replaced by a simple lever which slid over an indent in the latch plate.

In the mechanical department, four thermostatically operated flaps were

added to the engine's fan housing to allow air to pass through the car's heater and defroster ducts as soon as the engine was started. The heating controls were changed at the same time, swapping the old single control knob for two levers, situated near the handbrake. One allowed heat into the front compartment, while the other gave the rear passengers heat too.

Although they were relatively minor adjustments, the redesigned master cylinder and brake-shoe supports promised reduced lining wear, better performance and the need for less pedal pressure. Other interior comforts included thinner, contored front seat backs, making it more comfortable in the front and more spacious in the back. The rear seat back also now folded almost flat, allowing you to carry a lot more luggage (as long as you didn't want to carry passengers at the same time!)

The official Beetle range was altered slightly in 1965 too. Standard, Export and Convertible – the line-up since 1949 – was changed to 1200A, 1200 and Convertible. For some reason, it was the Standard that gained the A suffix, even though it was less well-equipped. It did at last gain the old Export model's external chrome, however.

One year later, the range grew even more with the new 1300 Beetle. The 1300cc was achieved by using the Type 3 1500 crankshaft to increase the stroke from 64 to 69mm. Bigger capacity demanded more cooling, of course, so they also increased the number of fins on the cylinder heads from 14 to 19. Other modifications like larger inlet valves, a bigger Solex 30 PICT carburetor and higher 7.3:1 compression helped the new engine to the magic 40hp mark at 4000rpm – enough to haul it from 0-60mph in as little as 23 seconds, and right up to 75mph.

From the outside, the 1300 Beetle looked the same as the 1200 except for the 1300 badge on the engine cover. All Beetles made the move to new ventilated wheel rims with flat hubcaps in 1966, while on the inside, the 1300 brought in one or two small changes. The new black steering wheel discarded the small thumb-operated horn-push and actually brought back the old pre-1964 half-ring. There was now a third demister vent in the center of the dash (also on the 1200A), and the sun visors now swiveled at the other end and could be unclipped and used to shade sun coming in through the side windows. The headlight dipswitch was now on the indicator lever and American cars even had an emergency flasher button which would set all four indicators off at the same time.

Exports had always been important to Volkswagen, but as the years passed, more and more concessions were being made to foreign markets, the USA in particular. Eventually, where improvements and modifications used to begin in Europe and find their way on to American models, now the reverse was true. The total number of Volkswagens sold outside Germany passed the million mark in 1966. The USA was still far and away the biggest market, but Ben Pon's European network was still significant with over 300 dealers. Austria imported 38,000 Volkswagens this year, narrowly beating Sweden at 37,000, Belgium at 30,000, Britain at 28,000 and Switzerland at 27,000. Although the company had many foreign manufacturing plants, the majority of cars were still shipped direct from Germany in as many as 65 freighters which worked non-stop. Ships were unloading over 1000 Volkswagens in the USA every day, returning with other cargoes, often American grain, coal or wood.

The company had set up their own sales network based in New York in 1955, two years after canceling Hoffman's franchise, and in 1962 they added their own purpose-built distribution center at Englewood Cliffs, New Jersey.

At one point, they did look at manufacturing Beetles in the USA, in fact they had even bought an old plant from Studebaker in 1955 for the very purpose, but at the time it was proved economically unviable. The USA did get its own VW manufacturing facility in 1978, but Beetles were never produced there.

The biggest foreign manufacturing plant was still at Sao Bernado do Campo, Brazil, established as early as 23 March 1953, with home production beginning four years later. From small beginnings – just 12 people assembling kits of parts sent CKD from Germany – the company had grown, until by 1966 they employed over 11,000 people and produced 95,000 vehicles a year, the vast majority being Beetles. Incredibly, this represented 62 percent of all passenger cars sold in Brazil and 42 percent of total vehicle production. At home though, Volkswagen lost its European number one position to Fiat in 1967.

On the styling front, the engine cover was restyled slightly and some cars gained pushbutton door locks, but that was about it. In the USA, they introduced the new upright headlights which brought to an end those classic sloping 'eyes' that had been such a feature of the car since its earliest days,

but the changeover didn't reach Europe until a year later. To find the changes for 1967, you had to look underneath.

Throughout the Beetle's history, enthusiasts had tried to make their Beetles go that bit faster, usually by swapping and adapting existing Volkswagen parts from other models. The new 1500 Beetle engine was another case of the factory following up on what engine tuners had already cottoned on to: the fact that the new 1500 Transporter engine would fit the Beetle. This new unit was more or less just the 1300 unit with the bore increased to 83mm to give 1493cc. Compression as up again to 7.5:1 and valves were bigger to give 44bhp at 4000rpm. The existing Solex carburetor was given an improved hot air supply system, ducting hot air to the intake and by now, top speed was up to just over 80mph.

The 1500 was a very significant model in many ways as it launched many new features in other departments, many of which found their way straight to the 1300. For a start, the new 1500 model had a shorter engine lid which appeared square at the bottom. It wasn't really square, but the larger flat area for the bigger license plate, as required in some countries, made it seem so. This engine lid was fitted to 1300 cars too, though the badge obviously didn't say, 'VW1500'.

Another first was disc brakes for the front end. The ATE discs became standard fitment on all 1500 models and continued on the later 1600cc ones. The 1300cc models kept the drum brakes but gained wider linings (45mm) and bigger front wheel cylinders (23.8mm) for improved stopping. A prime example of how improvements to the Beetle had become USA-led was that American regulations had demanded dual-circuit brakes, so they were introduced for both 1300 and 1500 Beetles in 1967 for the USA, but a year later for the rest of the world. 1200cc models had to wait until 1970.

Both the USA and Europe got new wheels in 1967, with only four wheel-bolts under the new flatter hubcaps that had come in a year earlier. The 1300 gained the same four-bolt fixings, but again the lowly 1200 had to wait until 1968, almost as if it was the melting pot for all the old parts.

Finally, the rear axle. In a final effort to improve the Beetle's handling abilities, softer torsion bars were introduced. And as the softer springing was not a particularly good idea when you had a full load in the back, they were aided by a new 'Z-bar' equalizer spring, which would only come into effect to increase the effective springing when the car was fully loaded. Rear track was increased by 4.5 inches at the same time and again, the 1200 followed a year later.

Little did anyone know it, but 1967 was one of the most important years in the history of the Volkswagen company. It was the last year under the leadership of Heinz Nordhoff. If the Volkswagen Beetle belonged to Ferdinand Porsche, then the Volkswagen plant and its staff belonged to Nordhoff. And as they entered the most important years of their company life, he would be sorely missed.

Above left: Flat hubcaps concealed the new four-bolt wheel fixing.

Below left: New for 1967, the 1500 with its distinctive engine cover badge, paved the way for many mechanical changes.

Above: In the late 1960s the new black interiors gave Beetles a sombre look compared with the whites and grays of earlier years.

Below right: The new 1500cc engine was basically just the 1300 with a bigger bore.

Twenty Million Beetles

The death of Dr. Heinz Nordhoff on 12 April 1968 spelled the end of an incredible era in German motoring history. Here was the man who had turned the tumble-down factory at Wolfsburg into one of the most successful car producing companies ever. A man who had masterminded from nothing the sales invasion of almost every country the world over, just by offering a simple little car that many people still poked fun at. And a man who had pushed, cajoled and encouraged his staff to ever greater and bigger things, not just by the force of his own personality but by the example he set.

Nordhoff had come from refugee (he arrived for the interview on a bicycle) to managing director at a single stroke. And even though he later admitted that he had not been a great Beetle-lover before he took over at Wolfsburg, he very soon wanted it to become the most successful car in the world. That he succeeded in this aim is undeniable.

Nordhoff had announced that he would retire on 31 December 1968 and had lined up Dr Kurt Lotz as his successor. When he died at the age of 69 some nine months before that date, workers downed tools to observe a minute's silence in tribute. Naturally, he had left the company in a strong position. Although production in Germany suffered a slight hiccup in 1967, dropping to 818,889 Beetles in total, it would top the million once again a year later. And worldwide production was still very much on the increase. From 1965 to 1973 there was only one year (1967) when worldwide Beetle production did not exceed one million.

1968 was a big year not only for improvements to the existing models but for yet another new air-cooled Volkswagen. For the Beetle, improvements began with the upright US-style headlamps, now adopted in Europe too. The new front end style also did away with the little horn grilles and coincided with a host of other exterior detail modifications. There were new trigger-release door handles, new, even bigger tail lights incorporating a reversing light, a pushbutton release for the hood and a new slotted grille was cut into the top edge of the hood for the new internal ventilation system. Best of all, instead of having to open the hood to fill up with gasoline, a new fuel filler was fitted, recessed into the front right-hand quarter panel with its spring-loaded flip-open cover.

For 1300 and 1500 models, 1968 also meant new bumpers. Some would say that over the years, almost every change in the Beetle's design was to make things bigger, bulkier and generally less attractive and these bumpers were a prime example. The new 'Europa' bars were both thicker and wider than the delicate blades they replaced. They carried no overriders either.

The interior saw a further new style dash with the fuel gauge at last incorporated into the center of the speedo. There was a collapsible steering column in response to American regulations (Americans also got high back seats with built-in head restraints), and there was a new fresh air ventilation system. Round knobs on the dashboard controled assorted cable-operated flaps to vary the amount and direction of the fresh air.

As any early Beetle owner will testify, its six volt electrics left a lot to be desired, especially in winter when bad starting, dim headlights and sluggish windshield wipers made life so difficult. Considering that most other major manufacturers had made the jump to 12 volt some years earlier, it was no doubt a great relief when Volkswagen announced the upgrade in 1968. American Beetles had, in fact, earned it a year earlier, but now the European 1300 and 1500 cars fell into line. The new 12 volt starter motor had a different number of teeth and therefore the '12 volt' engines came with a different flywheel to match.

Another introduction of some significance for 1968 was the semi-automatic transmission, significant not just in itself, but because the 1500 version (it was offered as an option on the 1300 in 1969 and 1600 in 1971), brought with it a totally new rear suspension design. The new system utilized double-jointed open axles and hefty independent semi-trailing arms which pivoted on bushes mounted to the rear torsion tube, near the nose of the transmission. It retained the old torsion bar springing, but improved suspension geometry by a sizeable percentage. The semi-automatic transmission was basically a standard gearbox with the first gear removed and a torque converter fixed on the front. A switch at the bottom of the shift lever actuated a conventional clutch via a small servo and you used it just like a normal manual transmission.

The new model for 1968 was the Volkswagen Type 4. (The company were never exactly renowned for their creative new model names.) Known as the 411, it was about as big a failure as the Beetle had been a success. An ugly four-door (the two-door was optional), the 411 carried a rear-mounted 1679cc air-cooled engine, somewhat like the Type 3 motor in design but actually a totally new unit. In time, there was a 412 model with a 1795cc engine and even a fuel-injected version, but neither of these sold in great numbers and production ceased in 1974 after just 400,000 cars.

Above: Despite light customizing and lowering, this Volkswagen Type 4 still shows that they were hardly the most beautiful of Volkswagens.

Left: Flat, upright headlamps, no horn grilles and thick new Europa bumpers – this must be a 1968.

Above right: Number 53. Will there ever be a Beetle as famous? Walt Disney's Herbie, in German livery.

Below right: The first official joint collaboration produced this, the VW/Porsche 914 powered by a 411E engine.

Previous pages: Beetles continued to pour off the production line at Wolfsburg until 1974.

If any good did come out of the Type 4 project, it was that the engine found its way into the jointly produced VW/Porsche 914 model. Considering that both companies had been born of the same father, so to speak, it was strange that it took so long for Volkswagen and Porsche to come up with a joint venture, and now they had, it was quite an interesting little car. The joint VW/Porsche company was set up on 11 March 1969 with a two-model line-up: the 914, using the 1679cc 411E (injected) unit and the 914/6 with the 2 litre flat six engine from the Porsche 911. The little sports car with its distinctive cut-off rear window was assembled at Karmann in Osnabrück, but the 914/6 engines were installed by Porsche.

By the time production was curtailed in 1972, the 914/6 had managed only 3360 units, making them very collectable today. The 914 lasted a few years longer, until early 1976, after 114,103 cars had been built. By this time, German Beetle production was at its absolute peak and total Brazilian output was about to pass the one million. The Brazilian plant grew at a fantastic rate in the 1970s, peaking at 230,619 units in 1972 and producing the five millionth car on 5 November 1979.

With Beetle production running at such high levels and Volkswagen obviously stretched to capacity in all directions, co-productions with other companies were very much in vogue. Yet another new model was produced in 1969, and unfortunately was yet another flop, in the form of the VW K70. The K70 was actually the offspring of a marriage between NSU and Auto Union, a merger which took place on 21 August 1969. The front-wheel drive sedan was produced at the new Salzgitter factory from late 1970, but lasted only five years. Only 211,151 models were built so very few, if any are on the roads today.

These new additions to the Volkswagen stable didn't stop the Beetle gaining the odd new feature. Neither did it stop it gaining yet another addition to the range. After the rush of 1968, the changes for the next two years must have seemed somewhat insignificant. The new hood pull (now in the glove compartment), the fuel filler flap, remote control lever, and the loss of the chrome dash trim, were only matched by the lack of new features in 1970

Above left: Seen here with more than its fair share of bolt-on goodies, a 1970 Beetle.

Below left: After 1968, the fuel gauge was at last incorporated into the speedometer. This US-spec interior has high-back seats.

Above right: The 1970 1300 is easily distinguished from the 1200 which still had the thin blade bumpers and sloping headlights.

Below right: A few aftermarket extras make the Beetle engine a touch more attractive.

when the 1300 and 1500 cars got a padded dashboard, an anti-dazzle mirror and deep pile carpets.

Increasing the Beetle line-up to three models, the new 1302 series was introduced in 1970 (for the 1971 model year). The three models, therefore, became the 1200 with its thin blade bumpers and old style rear lights, the 1300/1500 with its Europa bars and fresh air grilles and the new 1302, a very different Beetle altogether.

The reason it was called 1302 was very simple. It was based on the 1300 Beetle but the number 1301 was already taken by Simca. To a logical German, 1302 was the next available number. To many a Beetle enthusiast, the 1302 spelt the beginning of the end for Porsche's original concept. True, it still looked like a Beetle, but by now those beautiful original curves had mutated into a rather bulbous shape with giant rear lights and little flow-through air vents behind the rear side windows (which they copied on the 1300). Function had now dictated the form of the Beetle, along with American regulations and the impossible search for 1970s comfort in a 1930s design.

The reason for that new nose treatment was a totally new front suspension system. Simply by swapping a new frame head on to the existing floorpan, the old transverse torsion bar suspension was replaced by two MacPherson struts, with their coil springs and integral dampers. Transverse location was by track control arms, while the front stabilizer doubled as fore and aft location, giving improved ride and handling, but increased front track, giving the car a wider turning circle. The new set-up also allowed the spare wheel to be recessed into the floor, increasing front luggage capacity by at least 85 percent.

At the rear, the old swing-axle arrangment also bit the dust in favor of the double-jointed independent system, introduced two years earlier on the 1500 automatic. Although this new suspension layout was used on the following 1303 models, even adding rack and pinion steering at one point, the old fashioned 1200 Beetle kept the torsion bar front/swing-axle rear suspension layout right until the end of German production in 1978. That the Beetle started and finished production with the same suspension layout must say something for the excellence and adaptability of the original concept.

On the inside, more Americanization led to a total of seven outlets for hot and fresh air around the dash area, two-speed wipers and hazard warning lights. US versions even had a warning buzzer to tell you if the ignition key was still in the slot when you opened the doors. It was about this time that Volkswagen introduced the L and S suffix letters. L meant luxury, so the L

Left: This badge combines three emblems very close to the VW enthusiasts' heart.

Below: The 1302 series, first seen in 1971 introduced the MacPherson strut front suspension giving Beetle owners 85 percent more front luggage space.

Right: The 1500 Beetle engine cover received horizontal slats for 1970, and small fresh air inlets behind the rear side windows.

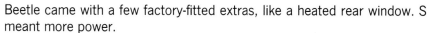

Beetle came with a few factory-fitted extras, like a heated rear window. S meant more power.

In 1971 the 1302S carried the 1600cc power unit that had been introduced into the American market a year earlier, while the normal 1302 came with the old 1300 engine. The remainder of the 1971 range was made up of the ordinary 1200 and 1300 models and in the USA, a 1600. The 1600cc motor replaced the 1500 to help reduce the negative performance effects of the tough new US emissions laws. US Beetles were by now sold under the 'Super Bug' name and the same year you could also get a mildly updated version of the 1970 model called the 'Custom Bug' with the 1600cc engine but a plain interior and no carpet.

The new 1600cc engine came with a stronger crankcase and bigger bores (now 85mm), but more importantly they had new dual inlet port heads. These had been introduced earlier on the 1600cc Type 3 engine and obviously required new inlet manifolds and a new carburetor, the Solex 34 PICT3. A bigger engine, producing more power, more revs (peak power at 5000rpm) and therefore more heat, it also benefited from a larger fan with new ducting giving the oil cooler its own separate air supply. With 50 horsepower, the 1302S was good for 80mph and had cut the 0-60mph time down to 18.3 seconds. The new dual-port heads and a 31 PICT-3 carb were also introduced at this time for the updated 1300cc 1302 model to give it 44bhp at 4100rpm.

A new four-spoke safety wheel with padded center was also introduced for the 1302 series, leading the way for a serious dashboard facelift in 1973. With its whole new style in non-reflective black plastic, this final dashboard gave the newly-introduced 1303 series a host of mod cons including rocker switches and a hooded speedometer, all aimed at the US market.

In Britain, the 1302S replaced the 1500 for the newly named Volkswagen (GB) Ltd. The British import company had already undergone one change of name in 1965 when it had become Volkswagen Motors, and would change again later in 1980 to become VAG (United Kingdom) Ltd, after the merger with Audi.

After some 27 years of continuous production, 1972 saw the Beetle break the Model T Ford production record when the 15,007,034th Beetle left the line. In the same year, Beetles were given a slightly deeper (4cm) rear window, giving it 11 percent better rear visibility.

The 1300 gained L trim and the engine got an electronic diagnosis connector that together with the proper Volkswagen agent's computer, could find 88 possible faults. There was a change to the Girling disc calipers and at last, the 1200 models were updated to 12 volt electrics.

Special edition Beetles were very popular in the early 1970s, and 1972

was notable for three of them, the GT Beetle, the June Bug and the Marathon Beetle. The Marathon celebrated the Beetle beating the Model T in terms of total production figures, the GT coincided with the 300,000th British Beetle and the June model . . . well, it came out in June. Other specials included the Jeans Beetle, with its bright yellow paintwork and denim trim; the Chocolate Beetle, a 1303 with brown paintwork and beige trim; the Sun Bug (available in Sun Orange or Sun Yellow); and to finish the Beetle line in 1978, a batch of 1200L models, called the 'Last Edition'. Further Beetles were sold in the UK, of course, but these were either Karmann-built Cabriolets or Mexican-built sedans.

As radical as it had been in setting a new style for seventies' Beetles, the 1302 was shortlived, The 1303 series, specifically geared to the US market, appeared in 1973 and made things worse for many Beetle enthusiasts. The 1303 may have carried the Beetle name but it hardly carried the original Beetle spirit. The body was again restyled to bring in a giant curved windshield, shortened hood and restyled rear fenders with the biggest rear light units it had ever had. There were four versions. Two 1300-engined versions, the 1303 and 1303L, and the 1600cc ones, the 1303S and 1303LS.

The Cinderella 1200 Beetle was still around, of course, and its fortunes seemed to change every year. In 1973 its chrome window trim was deleted, but in 1974 it went back upmarket with new L trim, the bigger Europa bumpers (even if they were black and not chrome plated), and the larger 1303 rear lights and wings. The 1303 went downmarket for 1974 as a new 1303A model came with a 1200 engine and basic trim.

US Beetles now had energy-absorbing bumpers and in line with their safety laws, the ignition wouldn't start without the inertia reel seat belts being locked into place.

After so much success over so long a period, it was almost unthinkable that Volkswagen could find itself facing possible bankruptcy by 1974. A loss of over £142 million, due partly to the world depression in the wake of the fuel crisis, but also to the fact that they had failed for so long to come up with the Beetle replacement, almost echoed the situation that Henry Ford had

Above left: After 27 years, the Beetle broke the Model T Ford's production record to become the most prolific car of all time.

Below left: One of three special edition Beetles for 1972, this is the GT Beetle with Apple Green paintwork.

Above right: The GT Beetle is distinguished by its sporty wheels, which were also available as an optional extra. A limited 2500 were built to celebrate the 300,000th Beetle imported into Britain.

Below right: Although they were fitted to the GT Beetle, these big rear lights were usually associated with the 1303. The car was based on the 1300s, but it came with a 1600 engine.

Left: The last Beetle to leave the line at Wolfsburg. The company had almost hit bankruptcy, but the new Golf would save the day.

Below: Despite new VW models like the Passat, the Cabriolet still flourished at Karmann. 1973 saw the arrival of the 1303 and 1303S Cabriolet models.

Right: This 1973 Beetle shows the new style 1303 dashboard, redesigned to cater for US regulations, with four-spoke wheel, padded fascia and fresh air outlets.

Below right: Four horizontal rows of engine cover slats were introduced in 1971 and stayed until Cabriolet production ceased in 1980.

endured in 1926. Fortunately, new models were in the pipeline. The Passat had been introduced in 1973, and February 1974 saw the sporty new Scirocco, assembled by Karmann. In May the new Golf was announced, which with the Polo (announced a year later), set the company back on the road to success. After so many years, trying to replace the Beetle with something similar was virtually impossible: the company's saviors were, of course, as far removed as could be imagined with front-mounted engines, water-cooling, and even front-wheel drive.

So it was that the Wolfsburg production lines had to forsake the Beetle for

the Golf. At 11.19am precisely, on 1 July 1974, the last Beetle left the Wolfsburg production line. Body panels were still produced at Wolfsburg, though, and cars were still built at Emden and Brussels. Beetles were still very much alive in the rest of the world too. The new Brazilian Beetle came with twin carburetors from September 1974. The Super Fusca (Beetle was called Fusca in Brazil) also came with rev counter, clock and reclining seats. But the end was never far away.

In 1975 more Beetles were squashed. The 1303S and 1303A were discontinued this year and the 1303 didn't last much longer. It was dropped in 1976, taking the 1300 with it, leaving just the 1200 and a low production luxury 1303 Cabriolet. By now the 1303 had bumper-mounted indicators, though the US spec cars retained the fender-mounted ones for 1975. To help meet the tightened US clean air regulations, these cars were also limited to one last engine, which lasted until US Beetle sales were curtailed in 1977 (it did last for one more year but only in Japan). The 1600LE came with fuel injection and, of course, a catalytic converter, necessitating the exclusive use of unleaded petrol.

As for the 1200, by 1976 it was more of a range than a model. The basic 1200A didn't come with hubcaps, but the interior trim was upgraded slightly with the 1303-style padded dashboard and four-spoke steering wheel, two-speed wipers with flick facility and two-speed fan. The 1200L came with the luxury of full headlining, chrome window trim and chromed bumpers with a smart central black strip. The 1200S came with the 1600cc engine, and the 1200LS with both engine and luxury trim. For 1976 only, the 1200S was even available with semi-automatic transmission.

'La Grande Bug' was the 1976 US-style Beetle — a real comedown from the previous years. Torsion bar suspension all-round and drum brakes were the new order of the day though it did come with a few items to make it a little

Left: The last German Beetle left the Emden production line at noon on 19 January 1978, though production continues in Mexico to this day.

Right: Brazilian Beetles, 1985 style. These Super Fusca models became the first twin-carb Beetles and came with rev counter, oil temperature gauge, clock and reclining seats.

Below right: One of the very last. A 1979 US-spec Cabriolet with 1600cc fuel-injected, catalytic converter-equipped engine.

more desirable including two-coat metallic paint in silver, lime green or topaz, sporty wheels and a rear window demister. For 1977, topaz was dropped for Bahama blue and the trim was upgraded to velour.

By 1978 it was all over for the German-built Beetle sedan. Chassis number 118,2034,030, a 1200 (not surprisingly), left the Emden line at noon on 19 January. The sign on top of the car as it left the line said 'Kafer (the Beetle's nickname in Germany) Made in Germany. 16,255,500. Production worldwide 19,300,000.' The only common part from over 5000 on the first and last Beetles, was the front bonnet rubber. The Cabriolet managed to hang on at the Karmann plant at Osnabrück until 10 January 1980, mainly to continue servicing the US market.

The end for Germany didn't mean the end worldwide, of course. In fact, production continued at several foreign Volkswagen factories for many years, usually as a hotch-potch of different parts from assorted years of German manufacture.

Although Nigeria had imported Volkswagens since 1953, it was not until 21 March 1975 that the company joined forces with the Nigerian government to build a factory at a village by the name of Ojo near Lagos. Home production began with 1300 and 1500 Beetles assembled from CKD kits brought in from Brazil. Many of these Beetles are used as taxis without a front passenger seat.

On 15 May 1981 a Brazilian 1200 became the 20 millionth Beetle produced, surely a milestone that few cars will beat. It was celebrated by a special run of 200 'Silver Bug' Beetles, painted a silver metallic with black stripes at the bottom of the doors announcing the 20 million, a logo echoed on the engine cover plaque and badges on the gear knob and key fob. Another interesting Brazilian Beetle, produced from the end of 1979, was the Alcool model, a 1300 version built to run on distilled cane sugar. Naturally, they required some modification to run on this local fuel, so compression was raised to 10:1 and the induction system was redesigned to incorporate the two separate carburetors on short manifolds.

Over the years, whether home produced or assembled from CKD kits, Beetles have been built not only in Germany and Brazil, Mexico, Australia,

Nigeria and South Africa, but also Peru, Portugal, Costa Rica, Thailand, Indonesia, New Zealand, the Philippines, Singapore and Malaysia, Eire and Belgium. Maybe this is the reason for its success. The basic Volkswagen design was so simple, it was suited to almost every country in the world. In Europe it provided cheap, simple transport for everyone from the working man to the company executive. And in the Third World it was able to go where many other cars couldn't.

The suspension has the flexibility and the versatility to help it over the roughest terrain, staying together where more modern, sophisticated designs would fail. And the simple engine needs little maintenance. It is not for nothing that Volkswagen engines and suspension form the basis for the most modern off-road racing cars.

That simplicity of design also meant that the Beetle could be assembled in any country in the world without massive investment in expensive plant. There are relatively few working parts and they can be easily understood by the car's owner. Anyone with a little mechanical knowledge could maintain and repair their own Beetle, not only saving on motoring costs (though the car's service needs are slight anyway) but helping to get them home in an emergency.

From the very start, Nordhoff insisted that every Beetle should benefit from the absolute best in aftersales service. Good product, good service, good organisation was the Volkswagen dictum. Wherever the Beetle traveled there would be a workshop skilled in Beetle service and repair. In the 1960s, Nordhoff even insisted on a service center in Moscow. They didn't sell Volkswagens in Russia but the German embassy had some and what if a Volkswagen driver was to visit Moscow?

Although it is now well over ten years since the last German Beetle left the factory the market for Beetles, their parts and especially parts to improve their look and make them go faster, is as big as ever. Far from forgotten, the humble Beetle appears to go from strength to strength, carried on the waves of enthusiasm for the little car from successive generations of young people. As Wolfsburg stopped supplying spare parts for the older cars, so small independent companies took up the responsibility. Surprisingly, most are in

the USA, where the automotive conscience and the will to restore a beautiful or memorable old car is so much stronger and widespread.

And more than just restoring cars back to (better than) original, a new generation are modifying their cars. Customizing is big business in the Beetle world, with set styles like the high-stepping 'Baja' look. With their huge tires and cut-back fenders, they look ready to compete in the toughest of off-road races. Alternatively there's the massive 'California-look' movement, started in the Los Angeles area, but now a style of customizing that is seen around the world. These lowered, loudly painted and usually very quick cars have again breathed new life into the age-old Beetle design.

The business of making the air-cooled Volkswagen go faster has never been bigger. At one time the Super-Vee single seat racing cars made the news, getting more power out of a Beetle engine than seemed decent, but nowadays its the off-road and drag racers that make the headlines. Admittedly, the most powerful race engines use virtually no original Volkswagen parts whatsoever, but the basic design is still there. And after all, when you're building a turbocharged engine that can manage the standing quarter mile in a regular 9 seconds (the record is around seven seconds) at a terminal speed of 150mph then you may be excused. The fastest standard Beetle over the quarter mile was the 1303S at 20.4 seconds.

In the history of motoring, no one car has generated so much enthusiasm, so many tall stories, and indeed so much love from owners of all ages. And few cars have generated such trust, earned over decades of good service, reliability and a longevity that is world renowned.

There has never been anything like the Beetle. And there will never be anything like it again.

Left: Fuel injection was required for all US-spec cars to comply with the strict emission regulations.

Below left: Mexican Beetles are still produced today. In fact, in 1989 growing demand forced up production to 240 a day with estimates of as many as 100,000 cars a year in 1990.

Right and below right: By the end of the '70s, the last few Beetle Cabriolets were all either black or white. The engines carried the endless pipes and valves associated with fuel injection and the fascia carried the attractive wood veneer trimming.

Above left: You won't see many Beetles doing this on the street, but on the drag strip it's typical. With over 200hp and all the weight at the back, it's hardly surprising either.

Left: The Baja style, built for off-road use with high-riding stance and cutaway fenders. Note the 'stinger' racing exhaust, sticking high out of harms way with no mufflers.

Above right: There are customizers, there are serious customizers and there are traveling works of art.

Right: Just when you thought that everything had been done to a Beetle, someone pops up with something new. This is the low-drag Beetle.

Far right: On the front of a Type 2 bus, the slogan that says it all.

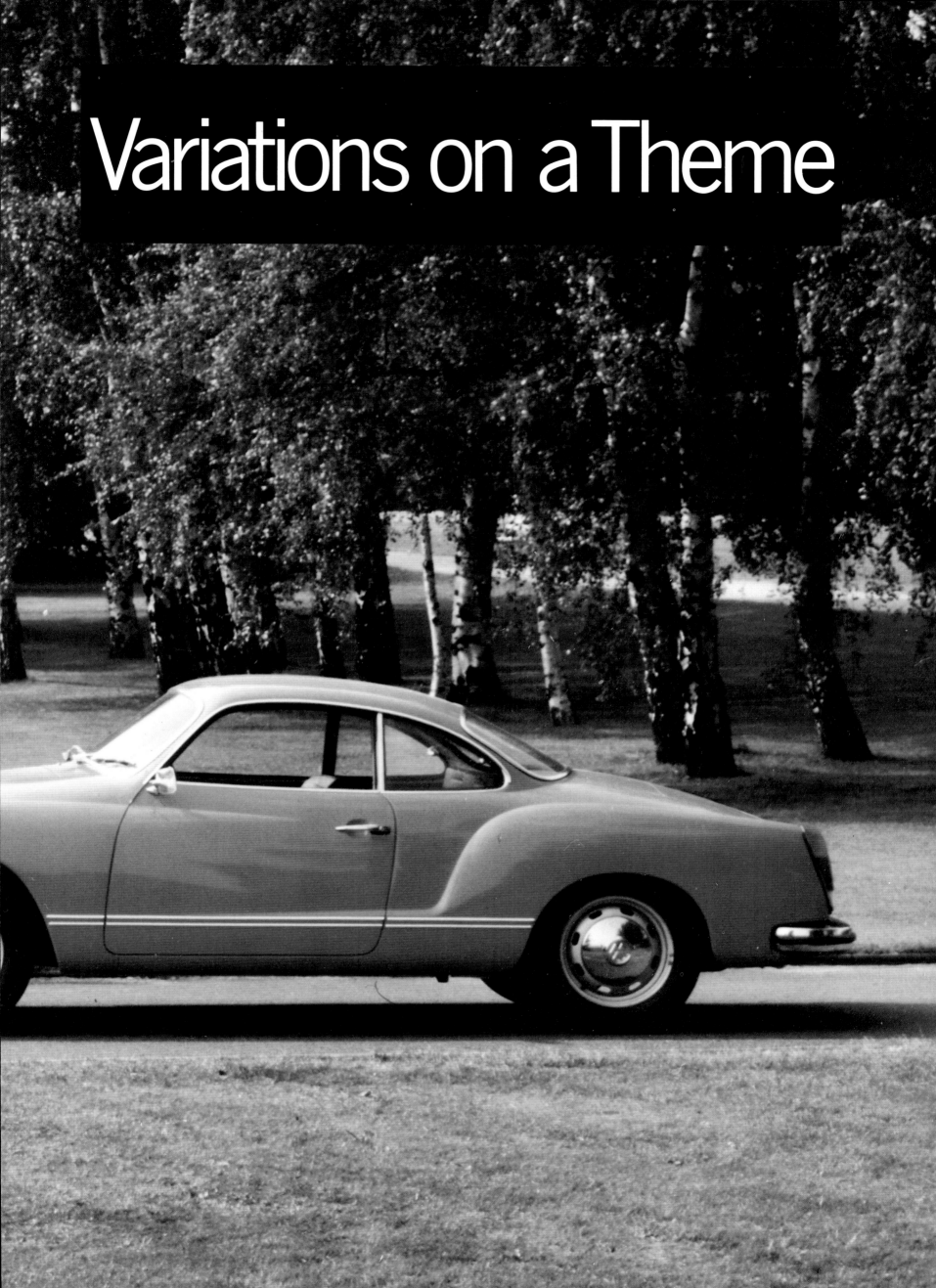

Variations on a Theme

A car built on a separate chassis floorpan that, with the possible exception of the fuel tank and the odd electrical component, would drive on its own, is a natural candidate for alternative body treatments. And needless to say, the Beetle has come in for more than its fair share. Little is remembered of the early attempts at bringing new style and versatility to the workaday Beetle design, but there were actually quite a few. Some were designed and built with the total approval and full backing of the VW plant, others definitely were not.

Examples of both categories include the Rometsch company who built several hundred four-door taxis and a very swoopy two-seater sports car. Another sports version was the Dannenhauser & Strauss. With its split windshield and very low stance, it looked very like the first Porsche 356 roadster. Franz Papler of Cologne built a four-seater coupé for the police, the Stoll company built a rather dumpy-looking five-window coupé in 1952 and Austro-Tatra in Vienna built some cabriolets used by the police and the Austrian army. There were also the official Volkswagen-approved models. Although the various Volkswagen sedans have been covered, the very successful Cabriolet model was available to Volkswagen customers for as long as the sedan – longer, since a Beetle Cabriolet was available right up until 1980, two years after the demise of the European sedan.

A Beetle convertible was envisaged as a valuable part of the range even at the earliest prototype stages, but it was only when Nordhoff arrived in 1948 that he put two versions out to separate companies so he could concentrate on sedan production at Wolfsburg. There were originally two Volkswagen cabriolets, a handsome two-seater by Josef Hebmüller and Son, of Wulfrath and the far better-known four-seater version, designed and produced for over 30 years by Karmann, of Osnabrück.

Using their previous experience in building a number of four-seater convertibles for police use, Hebmüller got round the problem of lost strength by

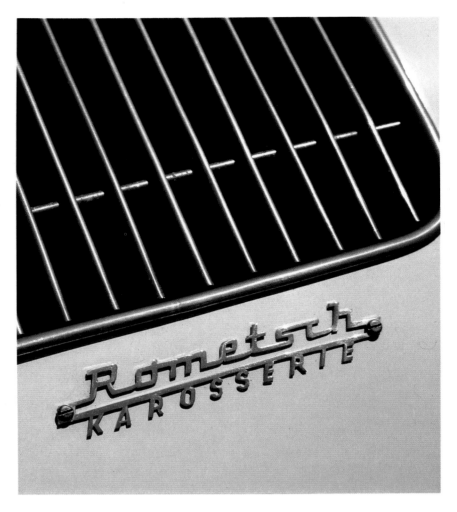

Previous pages: The beautiful Karmann Ghia coupé, seen here in late Europa-bumpered guise.

Left: The Rometsch company produced a few Beetle-based specials in the early days, plus a number of four-door taxis.

Below left: One of the best looking of Beetle-based specials, the Dannenhauser & Strauss roadster.

Right: The first official Beetle Cabriolets, this two-seater was produced by Hebmüller and Son of Wulfrath.

Below right: The Rometsch roadster didn't have the Porsche-style lines of the Dannenhauser and Strauss, but it was nonetheless a stylish looking car.

Left: Produced in the late '40s, the four-seater police car paved the way for Hebmüller's involvement in the Volkswagen-approved two-seater convertible.

Below: No doors provided quick, easy access, the auxiliary front spotlights made for better vision and the wind-fenders provided a little extra protection for driver and passengers.

Right: Grooved bumpers prove the car is pre-1952, but thin banana-shaped overriders place it even earlier at 1947/48.

Far right: When it rains all you do is close the doors, lift the hood and pin up all the side-screens. By which time, it's probably stopped raining.

designing a new windshield surround and incorporating two Z-section girders under the floorpan. The most striking aspect of the car's appearance was that the rear deck looked (and probably was to begin with) like it had begun life as a Beetle hood. Colonel Radclyffe had asked the Wolfsburg staff to build him a cabriolet back in 1946, and this was undoubtedly the model for Hebmüller's design, though it has to be said that the later example had much better lines.

After a tough Volkswagen test program of some 10,000kms, Nordhoff ordered 2000 of the new Type 14A, as it was called, and the model was launched at the Geneva Salon in the spring of 1949. With its natty two-tone paintwork (black and ivory, yellow and tan or red and ivory) and neat curved top, there was no denying that this was always the most attractive of Volkswagens. It was a pity then, that production of the Hebmüller Cabriolet was so shortlived. After a serious factory fire, which slowed production from the start, output reached a peak of 125 in January 1950 and then fell sharply.

According to Volkswagen records, the last Hebmüller left the factory in February 1953, though by then it was actually the Karmann factory as they had taken over the few remaining bodies once Josef Hebmüller had gone into liquidation in 1952. Company records claim a total of only 696 units, though the international Hebmüller Register has since brought this total into some doubt. One reason put forward for the Hebmüller Cabriolet's lack of success is the launch of the Karmann four-seater version, which may not

Above: Who needs living space when you've got one of the few remaining 1949 Hebmüller Cabriolets and a giant garage?

Left: From the front, you'd hardly know this rare two-seater Hebmüller Cabriolet from the four-seater Karmann version . . .

Right: . . . But when you look at the back, all is revealed. This engine cover looks more like the hood.

Right and left: Hebmüller replaced much of the strength in the Volkswagen bodyshell by building their own stronger windshield surround and placing two Z-section girders beneath the floor. Although Wolfsburg ordered 2000, a fire at the factory and later the fall-off in demand meant that far fewer than half that number were ever produced. There are fewer than 100 remaining today.

have been as good looking as the Hebmüller version, but was still quite stylish and so much more practical.

Karmann were coachbuilders in the most literal sense. Established in 1901 building horsedrawn carriages, they had been manufacturing simple car bodies from the very earliest days of motoring. In the 1920s they had moved over to proper steel body construction and by the 1930s used American moving line assembly methods, producing cabriolets for a whole list of European customers.

Karmann had approached Volkswagen with the idea of a convertible Beetle some time before 1948, but it was not until then that Nordhoff had given them the green light. As Karmann were contracted for a four-seater version, the modifications necessary were far less extensive compared with the Hebmüllers'. The roof and door tops were cut off, the doors and sills were strengthened and the floorpan was given much the same treatment. The lined hood was a strong vinyl material with a softer headliner and an inch of thick padding originally made of rubber and horsehair, but later foam. And to keep ample room for the four passengers when the hood was down, it folded

right back to sit, pramlike, around the rear body section. To ensure the engine now got its rightful supply of fresh air, new 'louvers' (though they were strictly cutouts) were stamped into the engine lid, vertical until July 1957, horizontal until July 1970. Right from the start, all cabriolets were based on the Export Beetle. They were quite expensive at DM 7500, though they were, for the most part, hand-finished.

With one or two minor exceptions, every modification and improvement to the Export sedan found its way straight into the cabriolet very soon afterwards, though the cabriolet often carried as standard what was optional on the sedan. The 34hp engine appeared in August 1961, the indicator signals replaced the semaphores (by then placed in the rear quarter panel just behind the door) and the new 1300cc engine arrived in 1966.

The 1500 followed in 1967, and in 1970 the 1600cc 1302S was produced in cabriolet form, only to be replaced by both 1300 and 1600 versions of the 1973 1303. Although the 1303 style Beetle was discontinued in sedan form in 1975, the cabriolet retained both the body style and the MacPherson strut suspension layout until the end in 1980.

Left: Contrasting heavily with the early Hebmüller, this 1973 Karmann four-seater model follows the sedan version far more closely.

Above right: When the curved windshield, 1303 models were launched, Karmann initially experienced problems forming a weatherproof seal with the top, but the problems didn't last long.

Below right: The Karmann Ghia coupé, introduced in 1956 featured twin air intake slats, which lasted until July 1959. Earliest Karmann Ghias were, of course, 1200-powered.

Below: The use of the MacPherson strut front suspension layout means that the spare wheel sits flat on the bottom of the front luggage compartment. It nearly doubled front luggage space.

Apart from the change in semaphore position and engine cover louvers, the main cabriolet-only modifications were as follows: the side window frames changed from polished aluminum to chromed brass in 1954, and in line with the demise of the sedan's oval window, the glass rear window in the soft top was swapped for a larger oval one. All cabriolets carried a small badge on the front quarter panel announcing the maker's name. In 1961, this changed from a square 'Karmann Kabriolett' (the first K used for both words) to a more curved, almost boat-shaped 'Karmann' version, with a six pointed star-like motif above the lettering. The only other change came in 1972, with a new all-steel hood frame, which reduced the folded hood height by at least 5cm.

In various other forms and engine capacities, the cabriolet outlived the sedan by two years. By then the vast majority of production was going to the USA, the cars were proving increasingly expensive to build and numbers were just not big enough to continue production, especially in the shadow of the new and highly desirable Golf Cabriolet. By January 1980 Karmann had produced some 331,847 Beetle Cabriolets.

Well known as the four-seater Karmann cabriolet is, the company's best known product will always be the Karmann-Ghia – the curvy, Beetle 'sportscar'. The story of how the Karmann-Ghia came into being and the question as

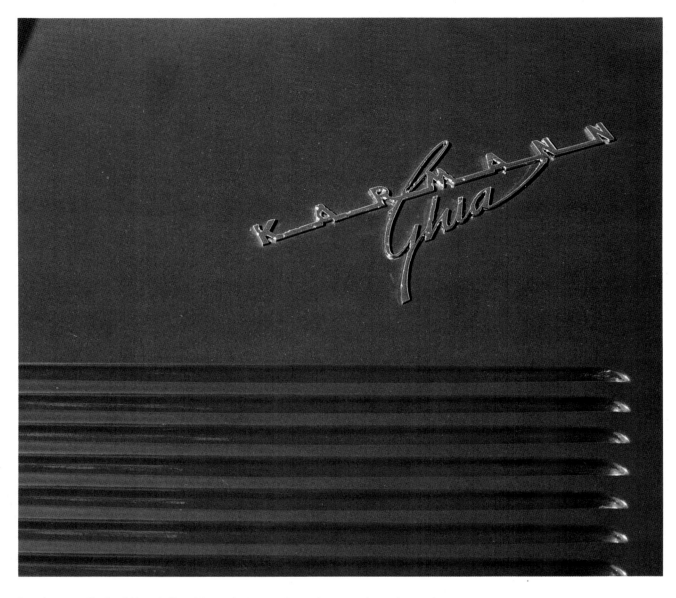

Left: Not immediately apparent, but an afficianado would recognize this as the engine cover badge on a Type 3 Karmann Ghia.

Right: The Karmann Ghia cabriolet joined the coupé in 1958. Later versions gained enlarged front turn signals and eventually, the Europa-type bumpers.

Below right: The Type 3-based Karmann Ghia was never as popular as the Type 1 (Beetle) based model, mainly due to its controversial angular styling.

to who exactly had the styling ideas that contributed so much to the car's success are to this day shrouded in mystery. While there is no doubt that the car was developed and styled at Ghia in Turin, the question as to whether those ideas were original, or plucked from contemporary Chrysler proto-types is only known to two men and they are both dead.

Dr Wilhelm Karmann Jr, then in control of the Osnabrück plant, had been negotiating with Wolfsburg for a sports convertible based on the Beetle floor-pan for some time, but Nordhoff stalled for almost three years, rejecting all Karmann's proposed designs. Eventually, Karmann went to Carrozzeria Ghia, in Turin, for additional input. Ghia, under designer Mario Boano and commerical director Luigi Segre, secretly obtained a Beetle floorpan (Nord-hoff refused to supply one) from France and presented a finished prototype for Karmann in 1953, though by then it was a coupé, not a cabriolet as they had expected. Not that it mattered either way. Karmann adjusted the de-signs slightly, widened the floorpan some 80mm each side and on 16 November, Nordhoff and Feuereisen (then VW vice-president in charge of sales) traveled the few miles from Wolfsburg to Osnabrück and gave the go-ahead. Within 18 months the first coupé was in production.

The controversy concerns the fact that at that time Ghia were also working for the American Chrysler Corporation, building their prototypes from Virgil Exner's designs and clay models. Exner was Chrysler's secret weapon at the time, having become head of styling at the prestigious Raymond Loewy Studio before pioneering the 'Forward Look' for Chrysler. According to Ex-ner, Ghia had previous designs rejected by Karmann until Chrysler asked them to build Exner's K310 and Coupé d'Elegance. The Karmann-Ghia was very like both, and if you cut the front off the K310, the similarity is extra-ordinary.

That wide swage line that starts just behind the front wheel cutout, run-ning back to the rear wheel then hitching up around the arch to form the top of the wing, was definitely a part of Exner's designs of 1951 and 1952 as were the heavily-raked front screen and rounded rear window glass. Boano's son, Gian Paolo (who himself later became head of styling at Fiat) claims that Mario had produced his designs in 1950, though we know that Karmann had not approached Ghia with the idea by then. The style was set however, and

for its time it contained many innovative styling features, some of which found their way straight on to the first production version. Curved, frameless door glass, that very wide (one meter) door opening, the high belt line, spring loaded over-center hinges and push-button door handles were all new ideas for the mid-1950s.

As Karmann possessed no big presses at the time, the bodyshell was con-structed from relatively small stampings, seam-welded together in water-cooled jigs to prevent distortion. These joints (there is nearly 12 feet of weld-ing in a Karmann-Ghia bodyshell) were finished with lead before the final paint was applied. As the contemporary advertising pointed out, Karmann Ghias were finished almost totally by hand, from the paintwork to the interior trim.

Although Karmann had wanted to launch the new car at the Paris Salon in October 1954, it was not until mid-1955 that the car was officially announced, though they did have to bring it forward to 14 July from 27 August because the Karmann plant had finished its last consignment of DKW Cabriolets and Ford Taunus Combis. Production was naturally slow to begin with, but storage soon became enough of a problem to warrant bringing the date forward. Once the car appeared at the Frankfurt Salon in September, orders flooded in. By December, production had hit 500 and only 14 months later, the 10,000th Karmann-Ghia rolled off the line.

With Karmann's experience in building convertibles and the fact that VW had originally wanted a cabriolet anyway, it was no surprise that an open-topped Karmann-Ghia appeared very shortly. At DM 8250, (a coupé would have set you back DM 7500) the new Cabriolet was announced on 1 August 1957. Although the car was based on the Export Beetle mechanical spec, there were one or two modifications right from the start. The Karmann-Ghia came with a front stabilizer for example, and because of the relatively low rear deck, the Beetle air filter had to be swapped for the remote Transporter unit, mounted to the side of the engine bay. The carburetor was rejetted to compensate. Incidentally, the engine compartment also housed the battery. For the most part, improvements and modifications to the Karmann-Ghia de-sign followed that of the sedan. The bodyshell changed gradually over the years to include larger rear lights and the larger Europa style bumpers.

Above: Production of the Type 3 Karmann Ghia was brought to an end in July 1969 after only 42,498 had been built.

Left: A low total production plus a fierce propensity to rust at alarming speed, means that there are few of these models left.

Above right: With its fold-forward windshield and simple construction, the Type 181, or Thing as it was known in the USA, harked back to the days of the wartime Kübelwagen.

Right: Based on the Karmann Ghia chassis, the 181 had reduction gears on the rear axle, causing it to lift at the back under acceleration.

Overleaf: Bumper to bumper – a VW enthusiast's dream.

In early 1962 there followed a Type 3 Ghia Coupé with its razor-edged styling, but it never really caught on and production was halted in June 1969 after only 42,432 of them had been built. The Type 1 versions motored on right up until 1974, when the production facilities were needed to build the Scirocco. Total production eventually amounted to some 364,398 units, of which only 80,897 were Cabriolets. Karmann-Ghias were also produced at the San Bernado do Campo plant in Brazil: Type 1 production began in 1962, with the cabriolet version arriving in 1968. Production ended in 1972 when it was replaced by the Type 3 based VW TC, a 2+2 coupé.

There is just one further Beetle-based model worth mentioning: the Type 181, introduced in August 1969 and first built at the Hanover plant. Looking somewhat like the wartime Kübelwagen, the 'Thing' as it was known in the USA, was conceived as a fun vehicle, though thanks to its basic trim and high ground clearance, a number were supplied to the German and Dutch armed forces. With its fold-flat windshield, boxy ribbed bodywork and basic canvas top, it was actually based on the wider Karmann-Ghia chassis and came with reduction gears on the rear axle, giving it that somewhat odd VW Transporter characteristic of rising at the back under acceleration.

There was even a British version of the Type 181, eventually named the 'Trekker' after VW had tried to call it the 'Thing' here too. Designated the Type 182, only about 300 were imported to Britain, however. In 1973, production was moved to the Pueblo plant in Mexico, where they also built a different version, with no doors in white with an almost comical Surrey top.

Finally, although there is not the room to cover the many Beetle-based 'kit cars' produced over the years, it is common knowledge that as well as being the world's most produced car, the Beetle floorpan has proved the most adaptable to other styles and forms of body. From those early fibreglass 'beach buggies' to svelte sporting models, even Beetle-powered Bugatti and Ferrari replicas, there have been literally thousands of Beetle alternatives, each as different on top as they were the same underneath.

Index

Acknowledgments

The publishers would like to thank Judith Millidge the Editor, Maria Costantino the Picture Researcher, David Eldred, the Designer and Ron Watson for preparing the index. We would like to thank the following agencies for supplying the illustrations on the pages noted below:

Bison Archive: page 11(below).
Bundesarchiv: page 12.
Colin Burnham: pages 20(both), 23(below), 39, 40(top), 41(below), 42(both), 43(top left & right), 47(below), 50(top), 54(below), 55, 57(below), 68, 71(below), 73(all 3), 78(top), 92(top), 93(all 3), 96(both), 97(both), 98(top), 100(both), 101, 102(both), 103, 107(below), 108(both), 109(below), 110.
Doyle Dane Bernbach Advertising: pages 60(both), 61, 62(bottom 2).
Mike Key: pages 44(all 3), 45(both), 46(top right), 50(below), 56(top), 57(top), 64, 65(both), 66-67, 71(top 2), 80(both), 81(both), 82(top), 83, 85(both), 86(below), 87(both), 89(below), 91(all 3), 104(both), 105(top).
Andrew Morland: pages 18-19, 22(below), 24(top), 46(top left), 92(below), 106, 109(top).

National Motor Museum, Beaulieu: pages 23(top), 24(below), 25(below), 36-37, 48(both), 49(both), 54(top), 62(top), 70.
Porsche Cars (Great Britain) Ltd: pages 8 (both), 9, 15 (top), 79 (below).
V.A.G. (West Germany): pages 1, 2-3, 4-5, 6-7, 10, 11(top), 13(both), 14(both), 15(below), 16(both), 17, 21, 22(top), 25(top), 26(both), 27(both), 28-29, 30, 31(both), 32(both), 33, 34, 35, 39(both), 40(below), 41(top), 43(below), 46(below), 47(top), 51, 52-53, 56(below), 58-59, 63, 69(both), 76-77, 78(below), 79(top), 82(below), 84(top), 86(top), 88, 89(top), 90(below), 94-95, 98(below), 105(below), 107(top).

Special thanks to the following VW owners:
J. Alexander
Phil Anning
Brian Clark
Derek Copas
Mike and June Key
Brian Lowe
Eva Miller
Peter Nicholson
Graham Smith
Robert Wynne